Chords & Theory

Major Chords

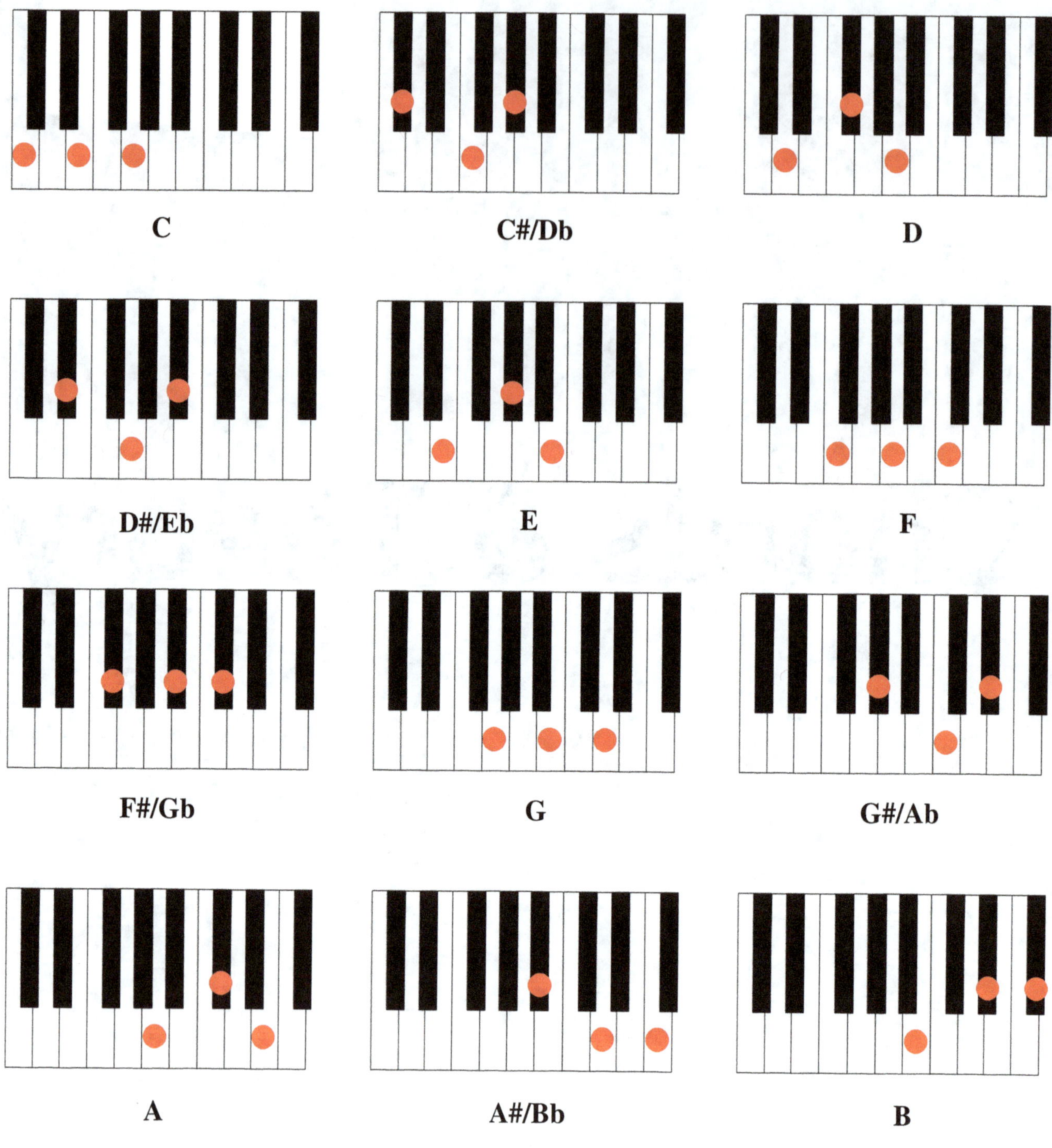

Minor Chords

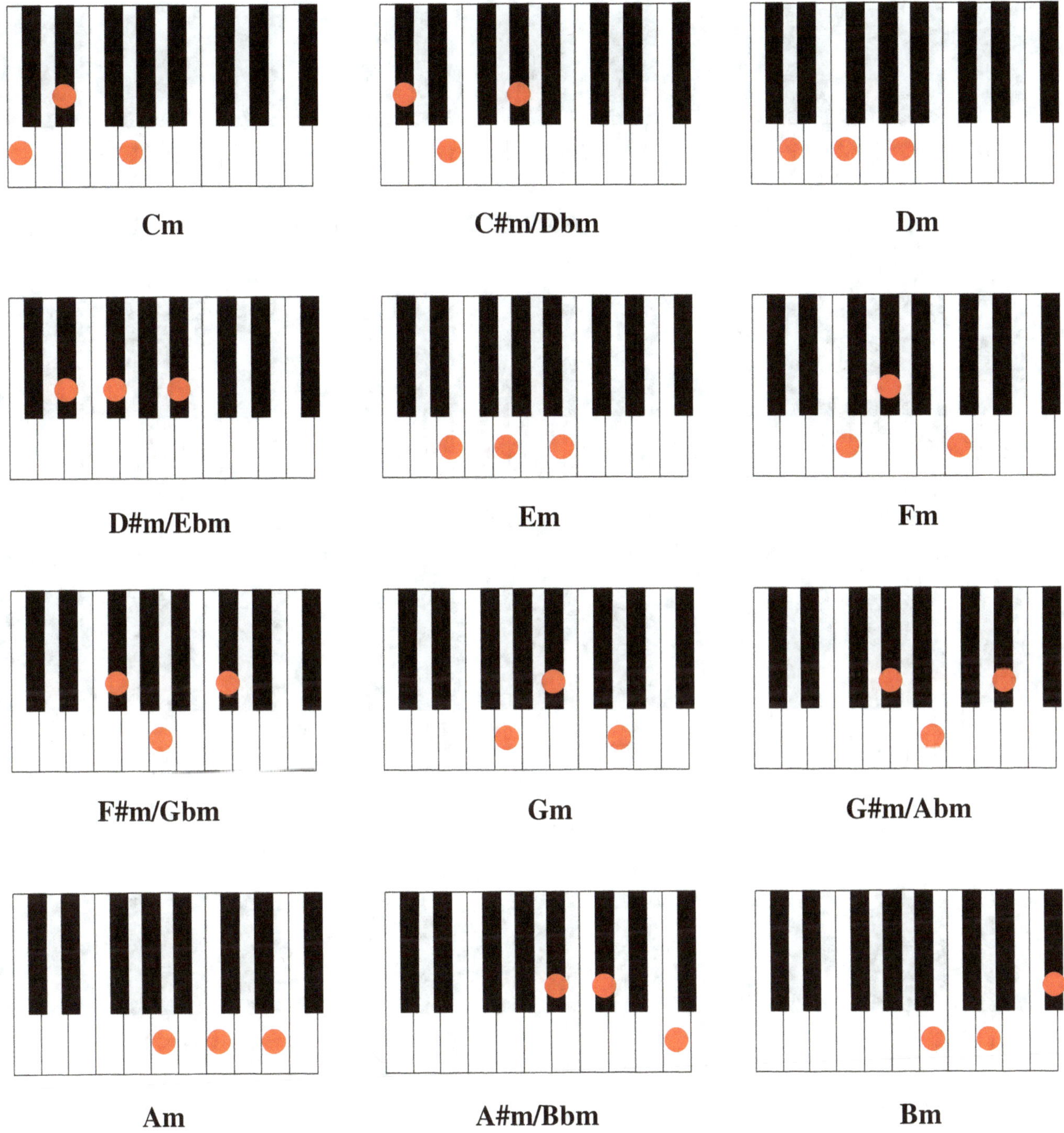

Seventh Chords

Augmented Chords

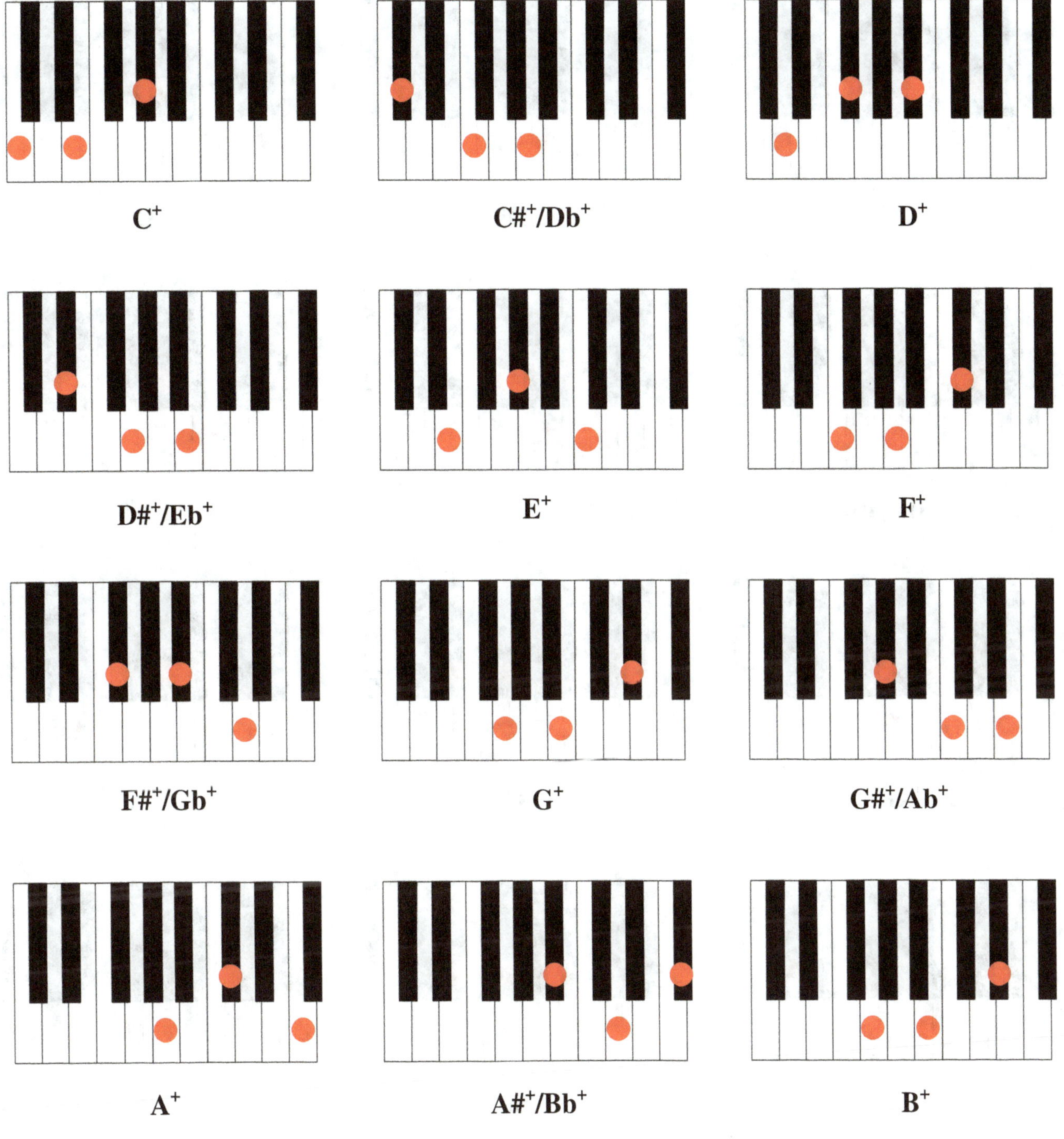

Diminished Chords

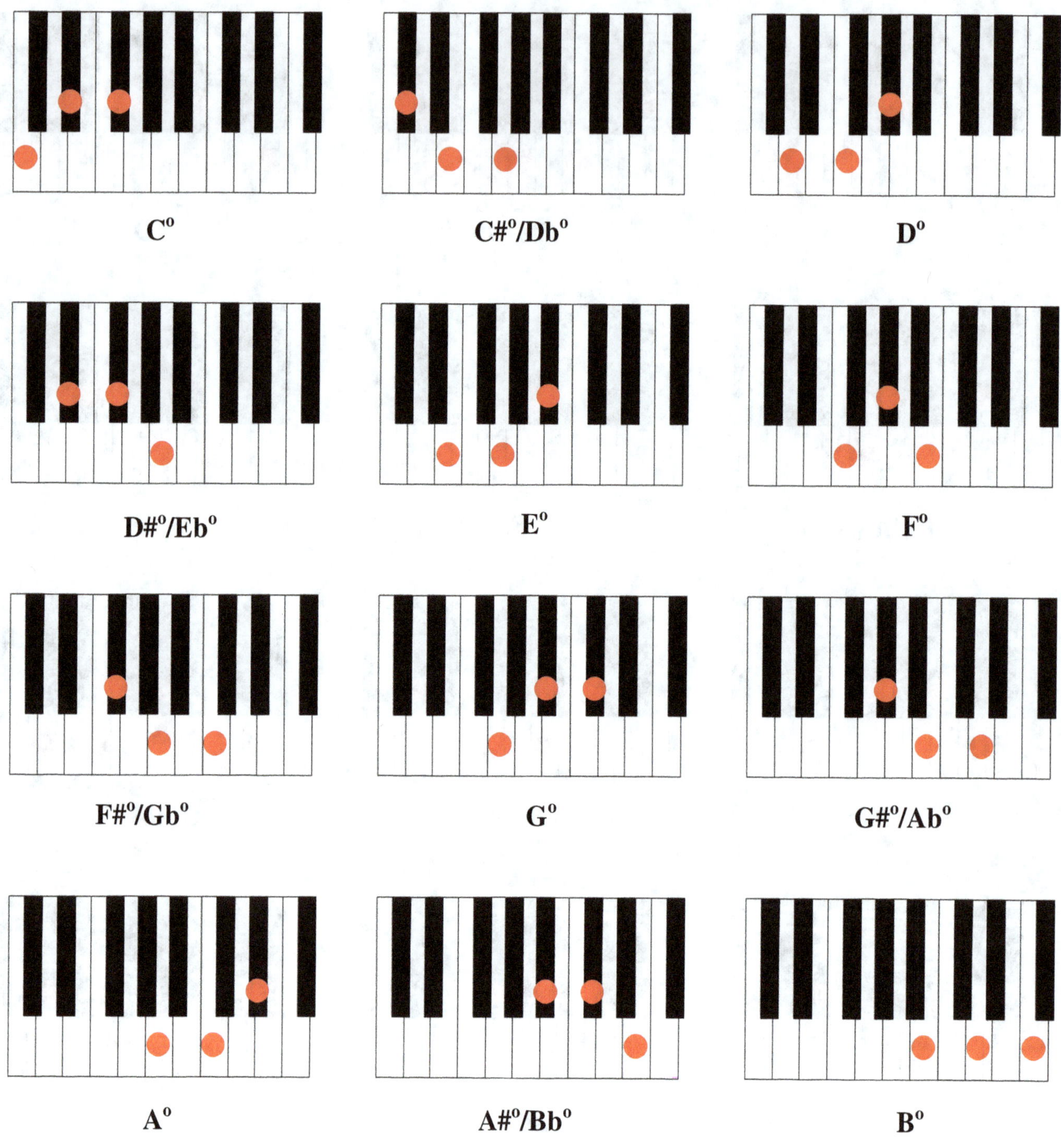

Piano Chord Voicings for jazz combo

The pianist has a few functions in a jazz combo.
First, he comps for, and interacts with, other players as they solo.

Secondly, he acts as a soloist himself.

Therefore, he needs two different types of voicings.

#1: TWO HANDED VOICINGS are used when other players solo and during the melody (often called the "Head").

#2: ONE HANDED VOICINGS are played in the left hand, while the right hand solos.

We are going to start with voicings for three types of chords: Major, minor, and dominant 7th.

Let's look at scale degrees for these three types of chords so that we can create voicings.

Understanding scale degrees

Lets look at the C Major scale.
We are going to number each note. We'll get the numbers 1-8.

When we change to C Dominant scale, we change the 7th to a b7.

Now, we are going to construct the scale for C minor 7th.
Minor scales have b3 and b7.

Throughout this packet, we will show you voicings in two
categories: Category A and Category B.
**We will call voicings with the 3rd of the chord on the
bottom CATEGORY A.**
**We will call voicings with the 7th of the chord on the
bottom CATEGORY B.**

We are going to start out with Major 7th voicings.
For C Major, our two handed voicing looks like this:

MAJOR 7TH TWO HANDED VOICING   Category A

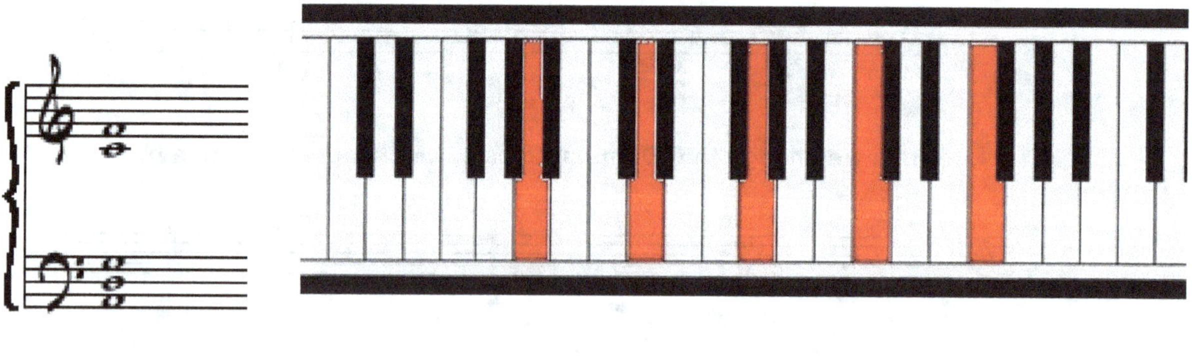

Tricks of the Trade
Put your right hand pinky on the root of the chord and continue DOWN in 4ths.
Or..
Put your left hand pinky on the 3rd of the chord, and continue UP in 4ths

Let's try the Major 7th voicing in one other key.
Here is the voicing for FMaj7:

To make a C dominant 7th voicing, or C7, we are going to change ONE note from the major 7th voicing: The b7.

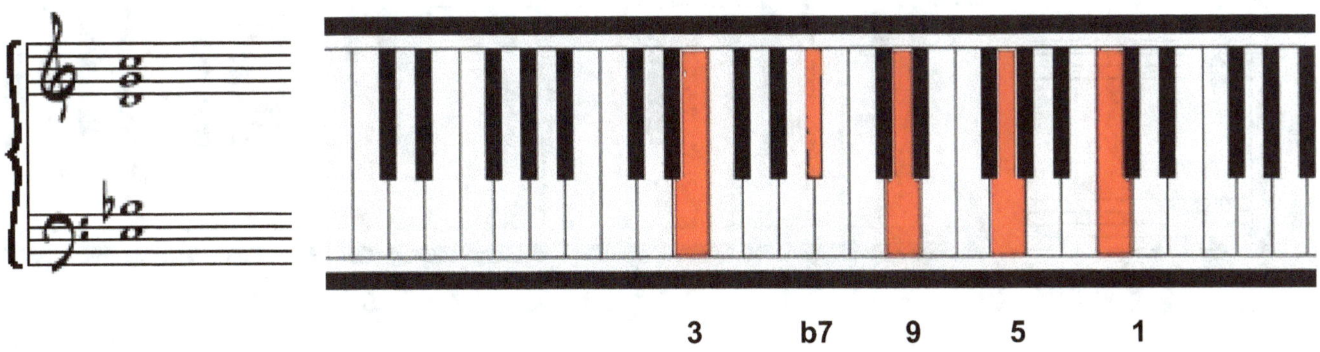

Notice that the only difference between the C7 and CMaj7 is that we replace the 6th (A) with a b7 (Bb).

Lets look at the dominant 7th voicing in one other key.
Here is the voicing for F7:

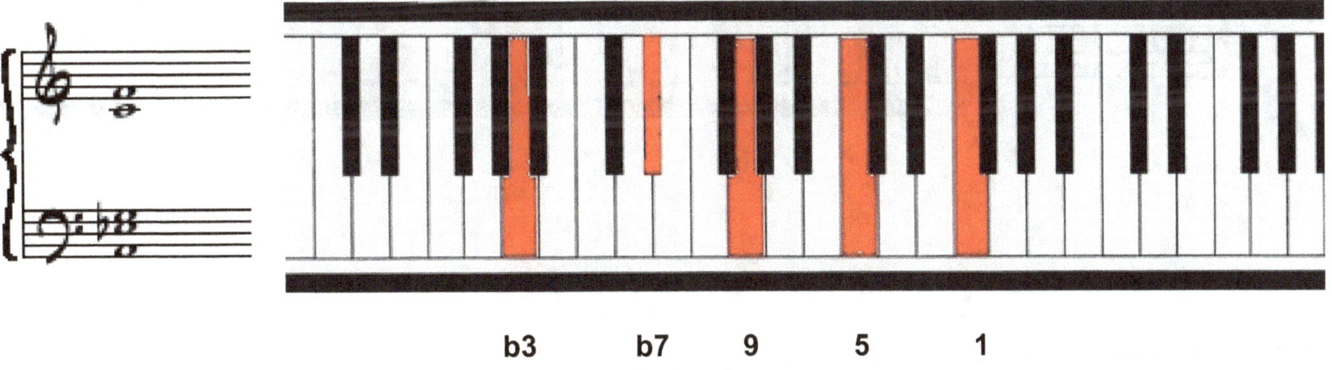

To turn a Major 7th chord into a minor 7th chord, add a b3 and b7.
To turn a Dominant 7th chord into a minor 7th chord, just add a b3.
C minor 7th, also spelled Cm7 or C-7 looks like this:

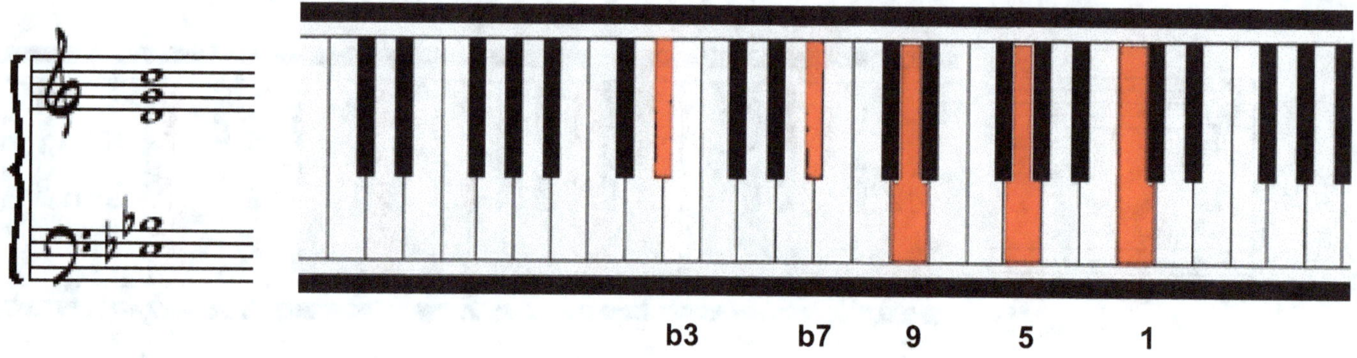

Here is this same voicing for F-7

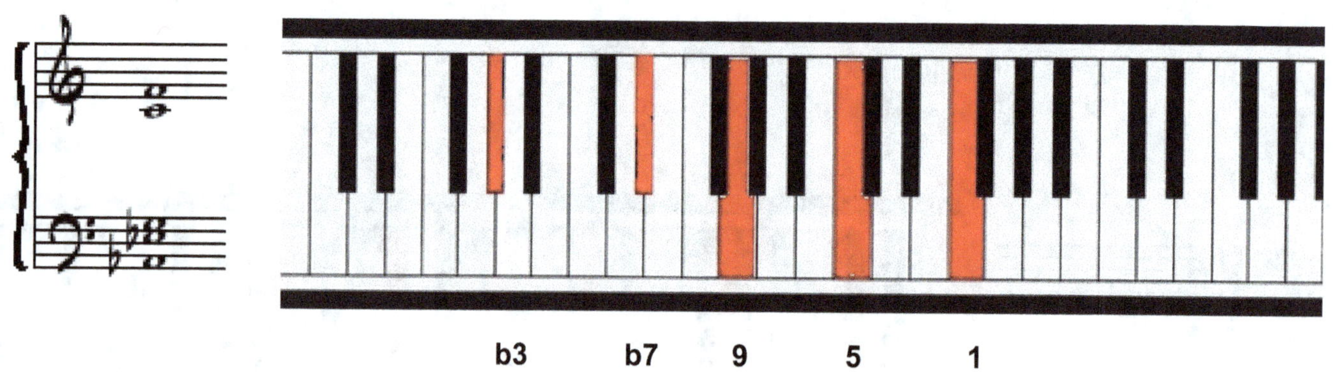

REVIEW

Comparing the three types of two-handed CATEGORY A voicings.

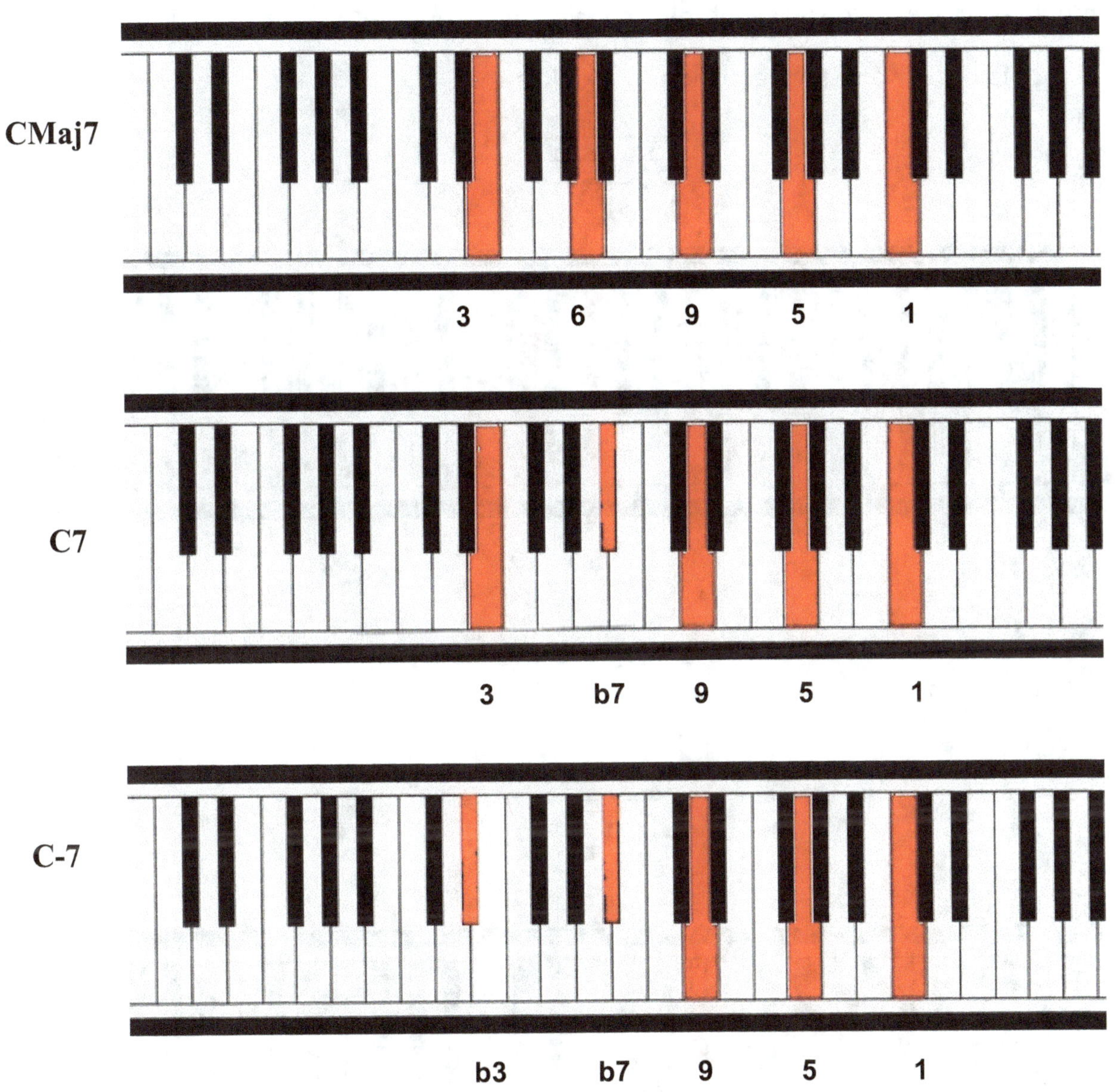

Remember, one handed voicings are played with the LEFT hand, while the right hand solos. Like our first set of two-handed voicings, these one-handed voicings will all have the 3rd on the bottom. These voicings can be played in multiple octaves. We showed it in treble clef below.

For C Major, our one-handed voicing looks like this:

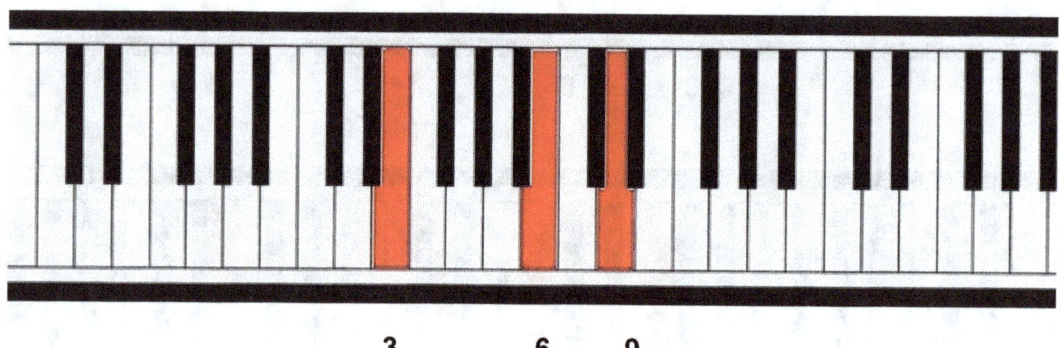

Lets try it in one more key, G Major:

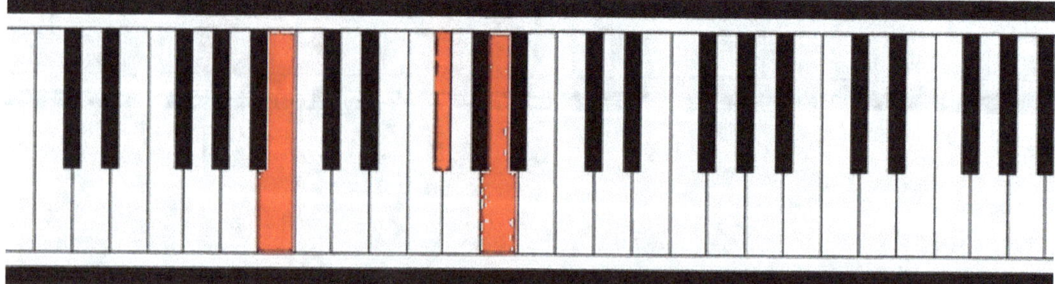

Remember, to change any set of notes from major to dominant, we only need to change the 7th to a **flat** 7th.

Our one-handed C7 voicing looks like this:

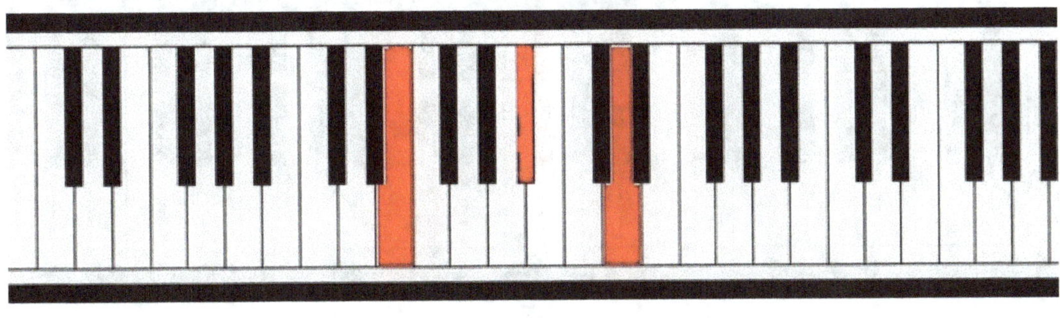

Our one-handed G7 voicing looks like this:

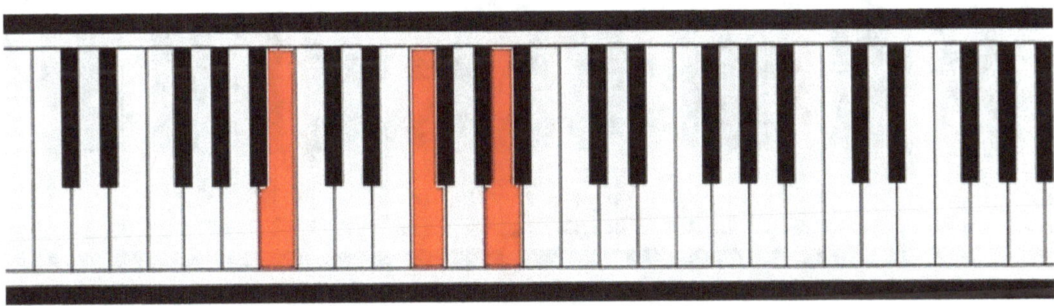

Remember, to go from major to minor, we need to flat both the 3ʳᵈ and the 7ᵗʰ.

Our one-handed C-7 voicing looks like this:

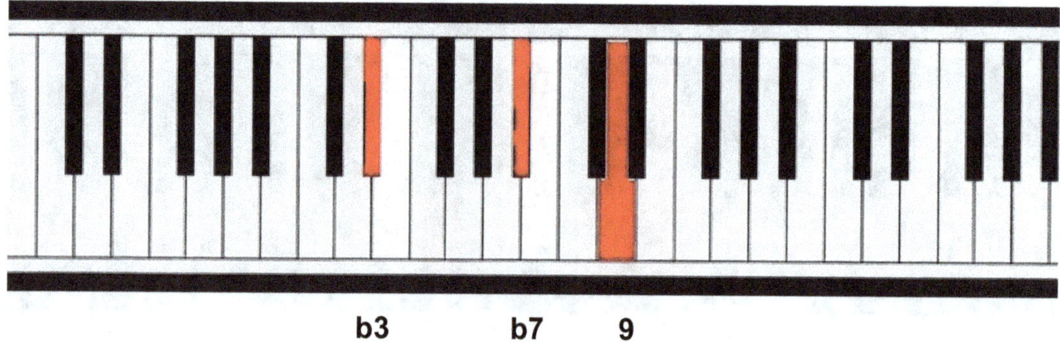

Our one-handed G-7 voicing looks like this:

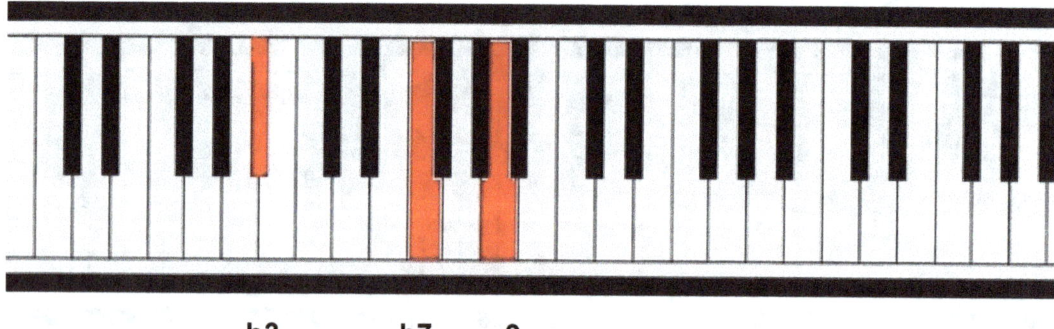

REVIEW
Comparing the three types of CATEGORY A one-handed voicings

CMaj7

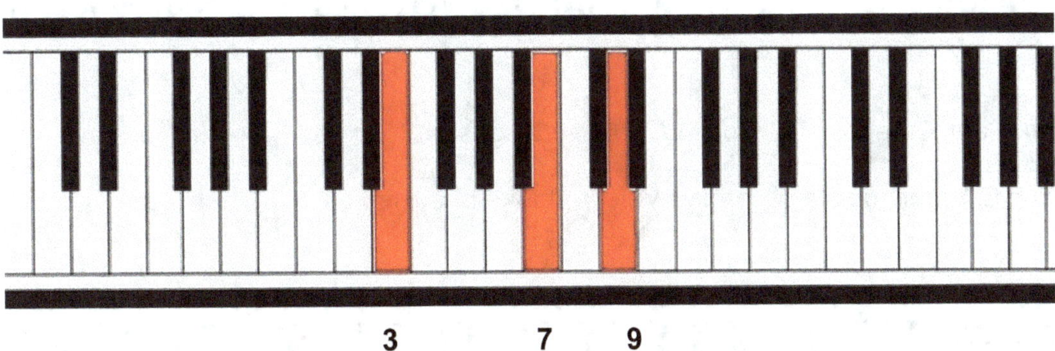

C7

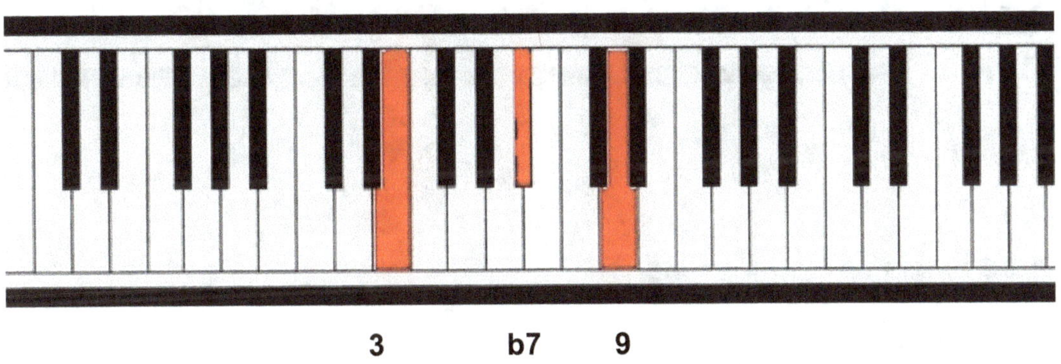

C-7

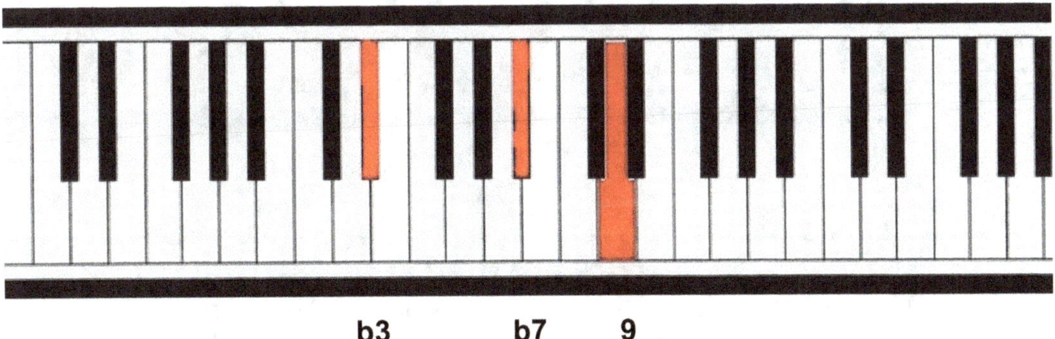

Category B Voicings

Next, we are going to move on to voicings with the 7th on the bottom. We are going to call these voicings **CATEGORY B.**

MAJOR 7TH	**TWO HANDED VOICING**	**Category A**

Like our Category "A" voicing, this voicing is all fourths.

For C Major, our two handed voicing looks like this:

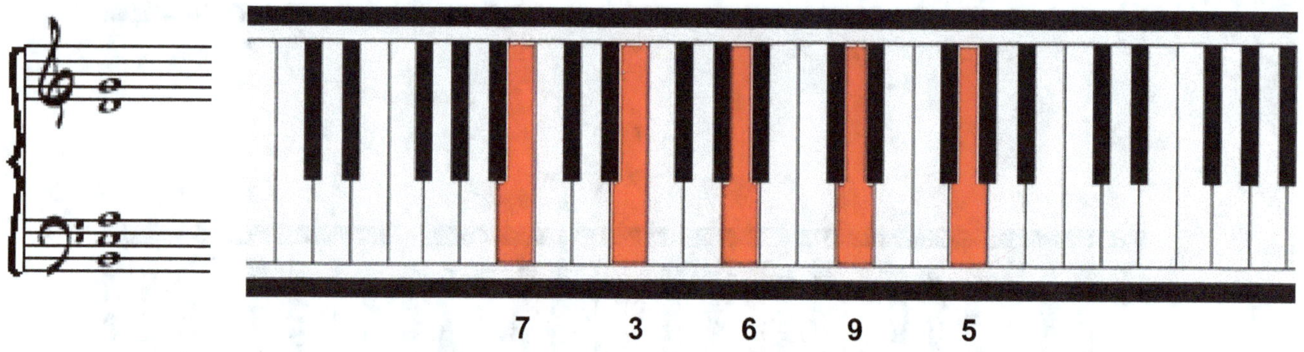

Here is this voicing for FMaj7:

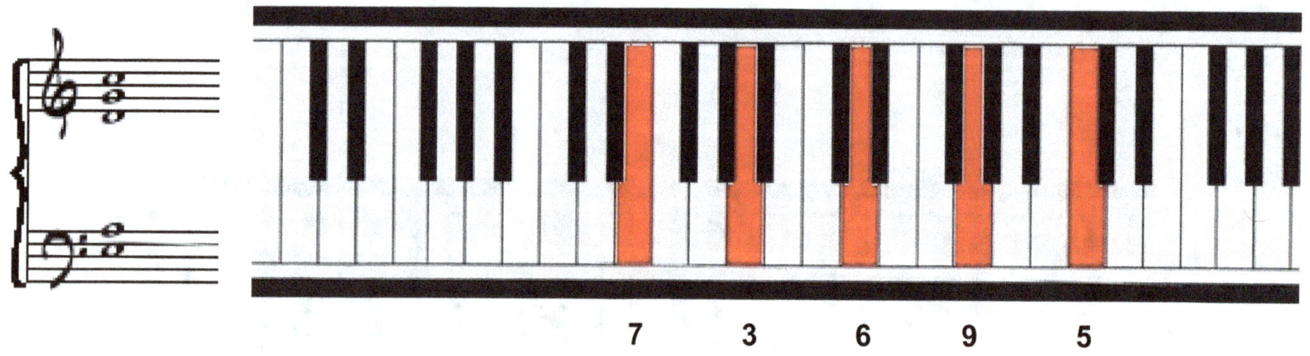

Tricks of the Trade
Notice that this voicing descends and ascends in fourths.
Put your Right hand pinky on the ROOT, and descend in fourths. Or,
Put your Left hand pinky on the seventh, and ascend in fourths.

Remember, to make a C dominant 7th voicing, or C7, we are going to change ONE note from the major 7th voicing: The b7.

Look at our C7 voicing.

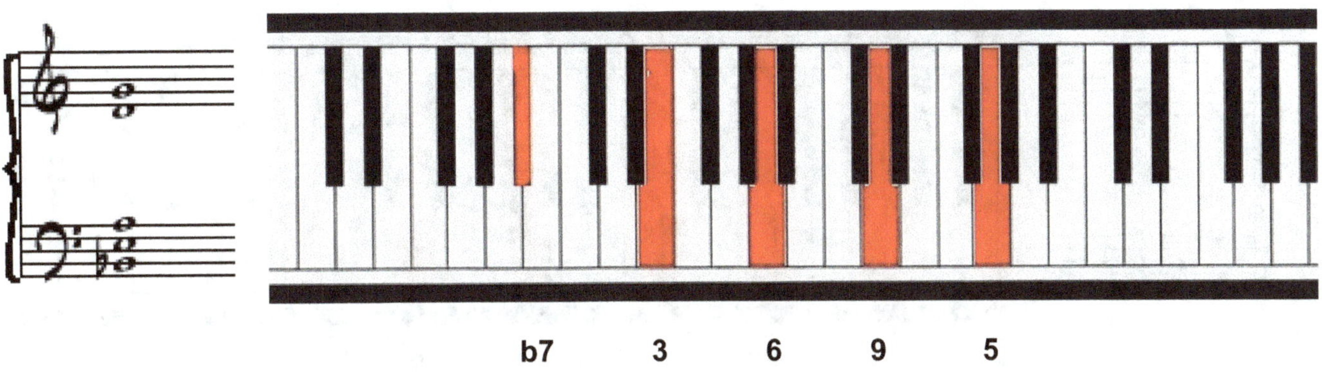

Let's look at this same voicing for F7.

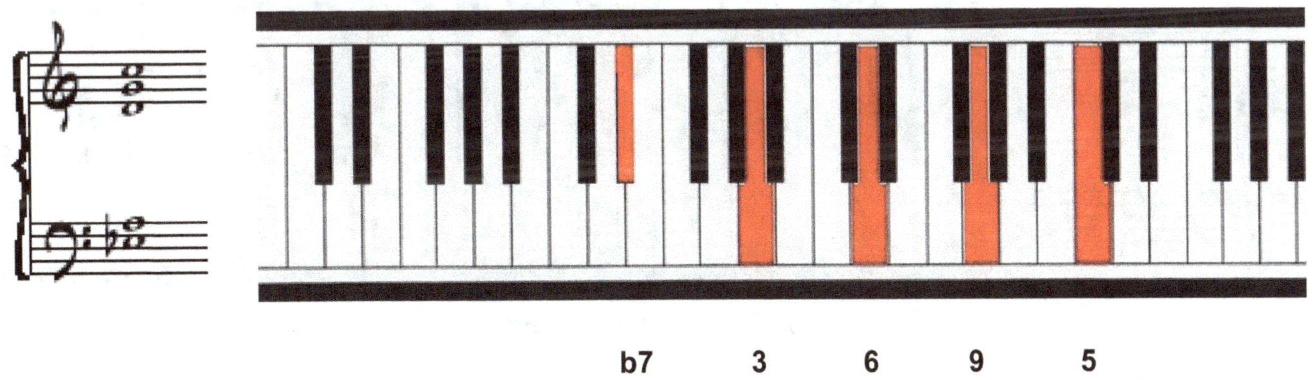

Tricks of the Trade
The right hand of this voicing is in still 4ths.
The left hand is on the 3rd and b7th.

To turn a Major 7th chord into a minor 7th chord, add a b3 and b7

To turn a Dominant 7th chord into a minor 7th chord, just add a b3

Here is the minor 7th voicing for C-7

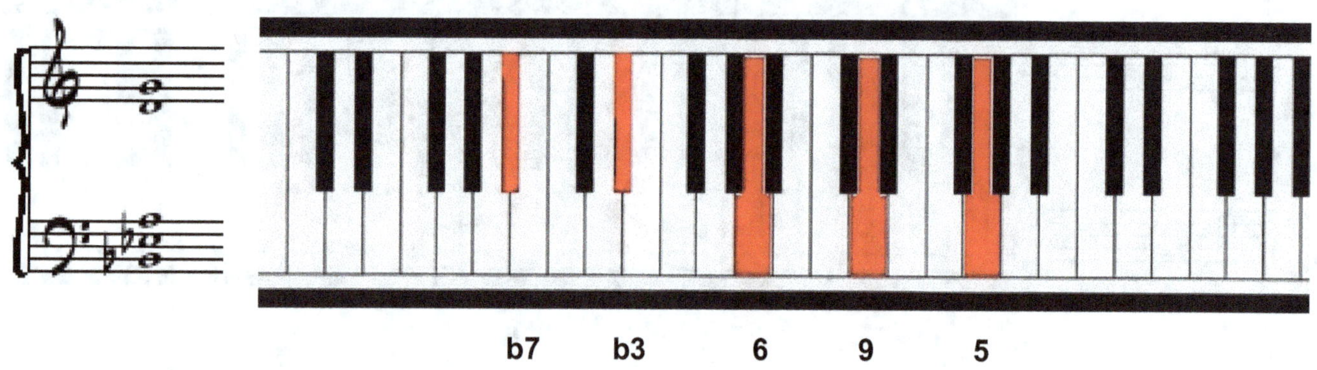

Here's this same voicing for F-7

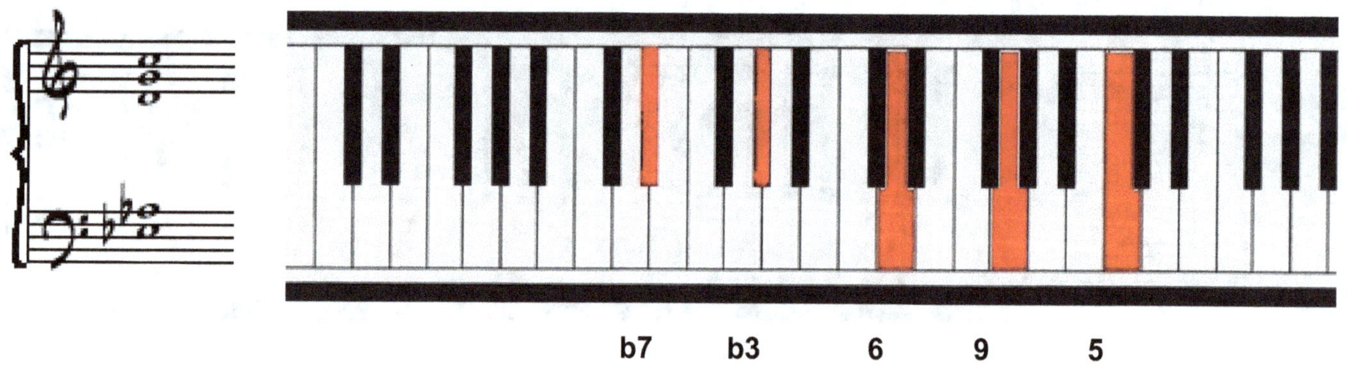

Tricks of the Trade

The right hand of this voicing is in still 4ths. The left hand is on the b3rd and b7th.

Practice Tip

Practice going from C Major 7 to C7 to C-7.
Notice that ONLY YOUR LEFT HAND will change. Do this in all the keys.
This is a great ear-training exercise.

REVIEW
Comparing the three types of one-handed voicings: category B.

CMaj7

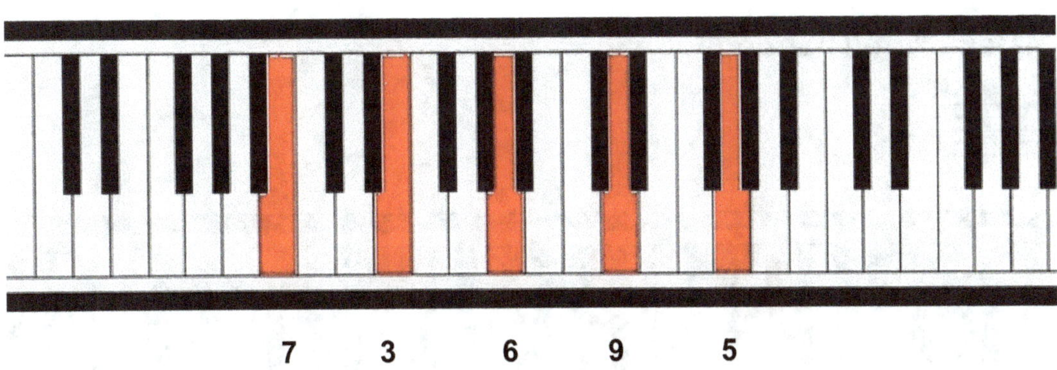

C7

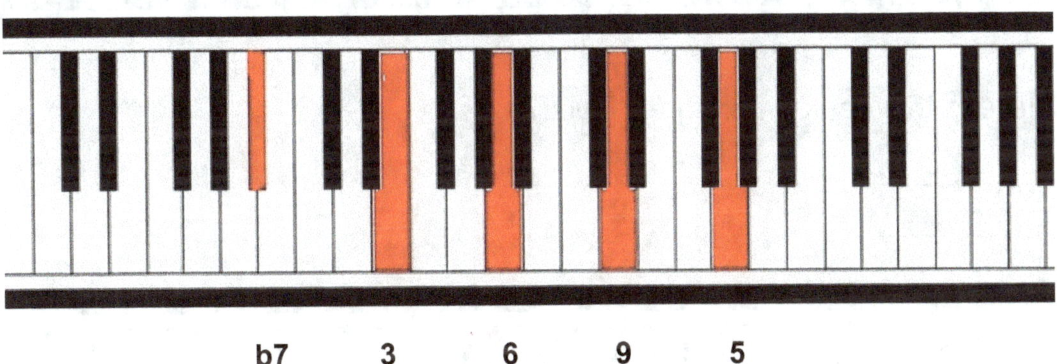

C-7

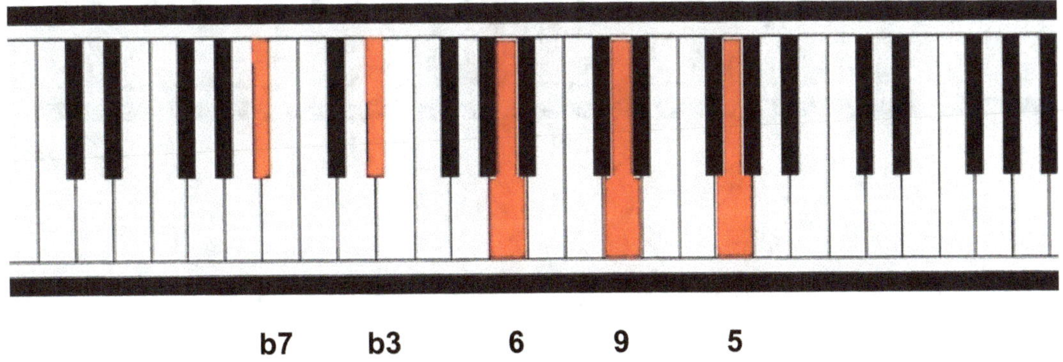

Now, let's look at our Category B one handed voicings.

Our Category B Voicings have the 7th on the bottom.

MAJOR 7TH   **ONE HANDED VOICING**   **Category B**

Major 7th one handed

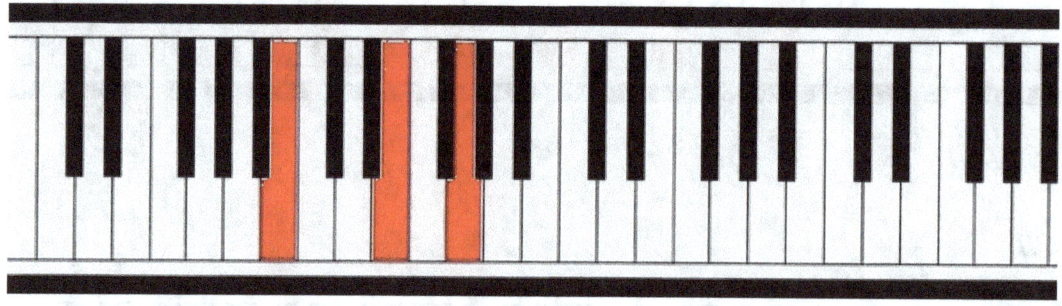

Here is this same voicing for FMaj7

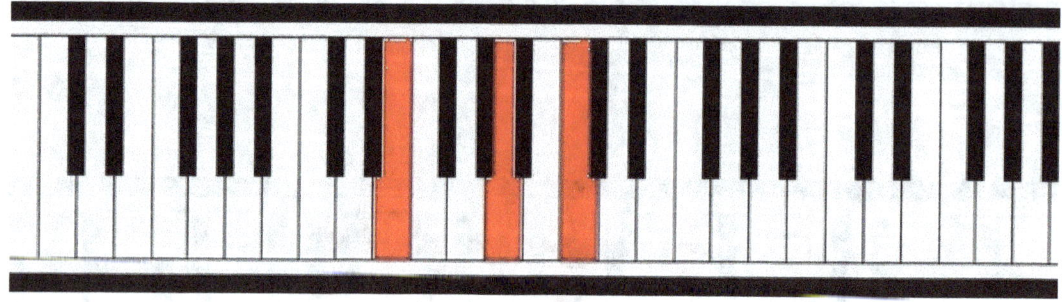

C7

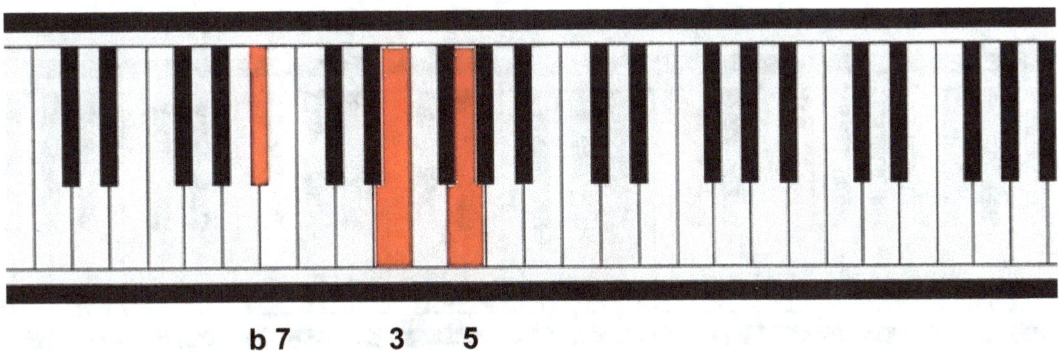

F7

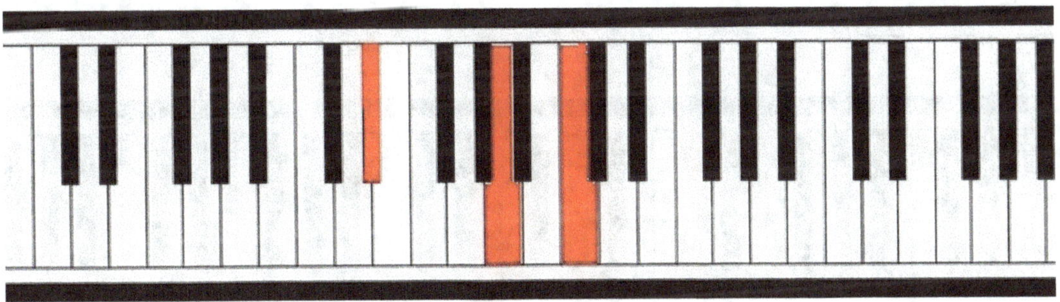

C-7

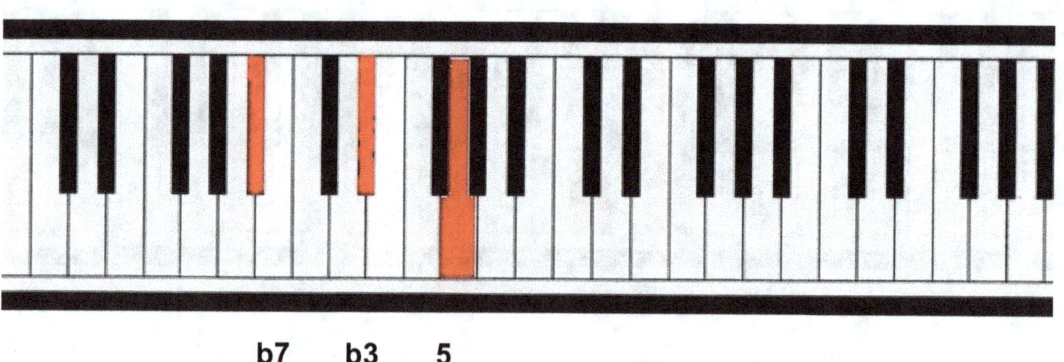

F-7

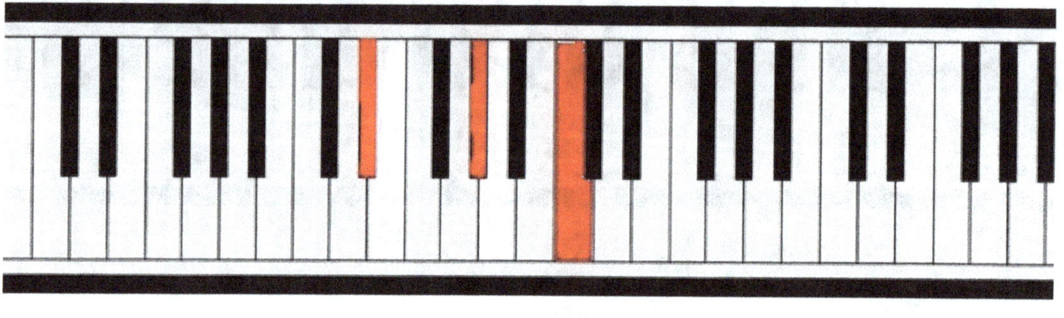

REVIEW
Comparing the one handed voicings: Category B

CMaj7

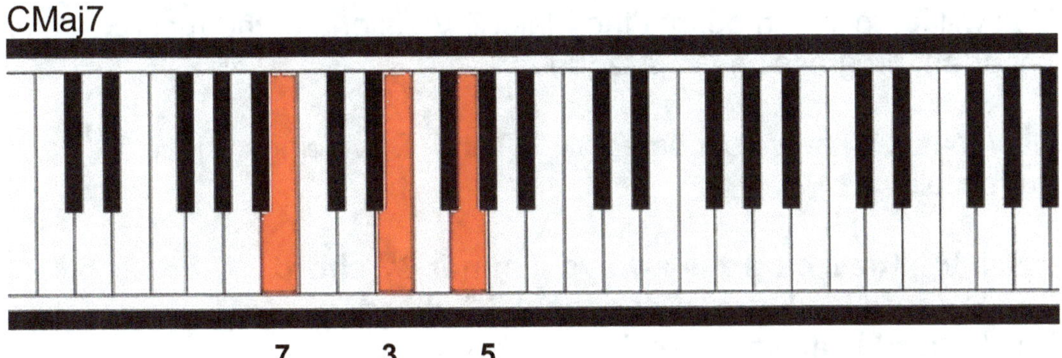

C7

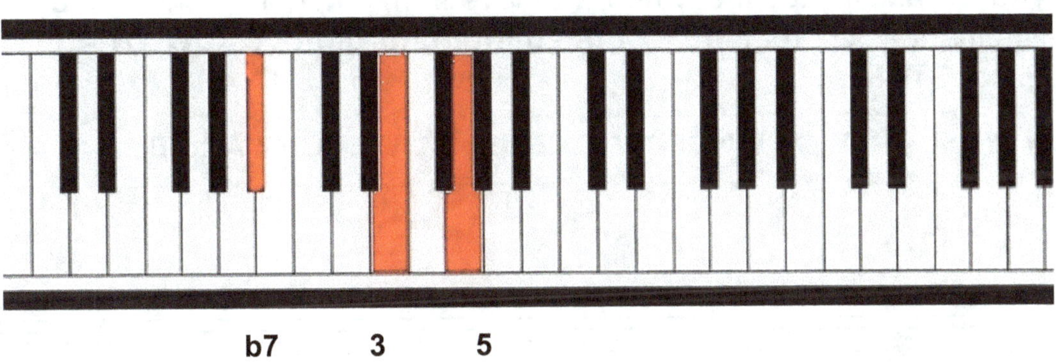

C-7

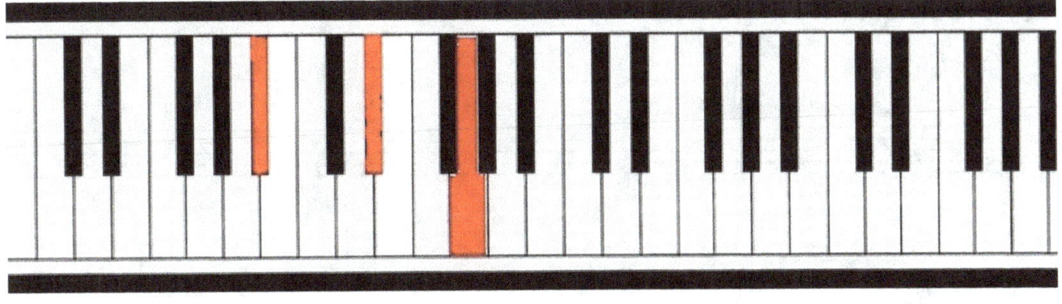

The Major ii V I

You will learn in combo that the Major ii V I is one of the most important progressions in jazz tunes.

Now that you know your category "A" and "B" voicings, these ii V I's are simple.

In a ii V I, the ii chord is always a minor 7th chord
The V chord is always a dominant 7th chord
The I chord is always a major 7th chord.

The trick to playing these ii V's is that we will always go from category **A to B to A**, or from category **B to A to B**.

You will also notice that when we move from a minor 7th chord to a dominant 7th chord, the **7th of the minor chord moves DOWN A HALF STEP.**

ii V I   TWO HANDED VOICING   CATEGORY A to B to A

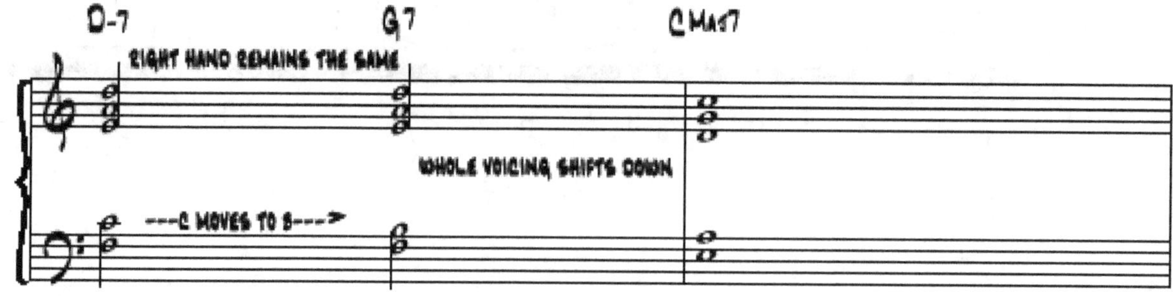

Let's look at a ii V I in F Major:

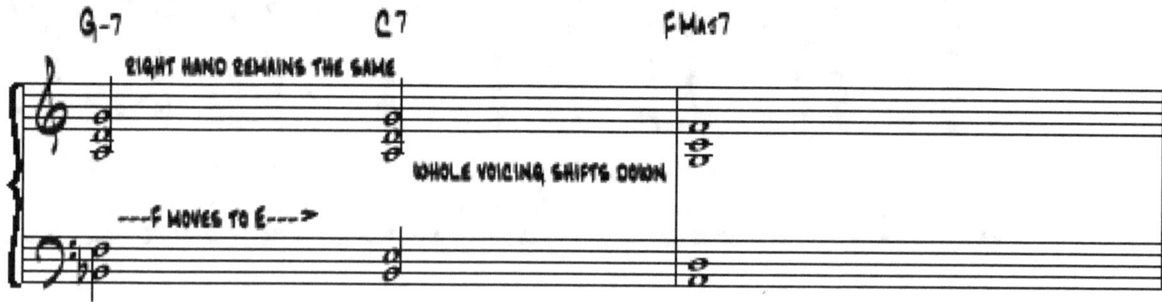

Now let's look at the ii V I again, going from category B to A to B in C Major.

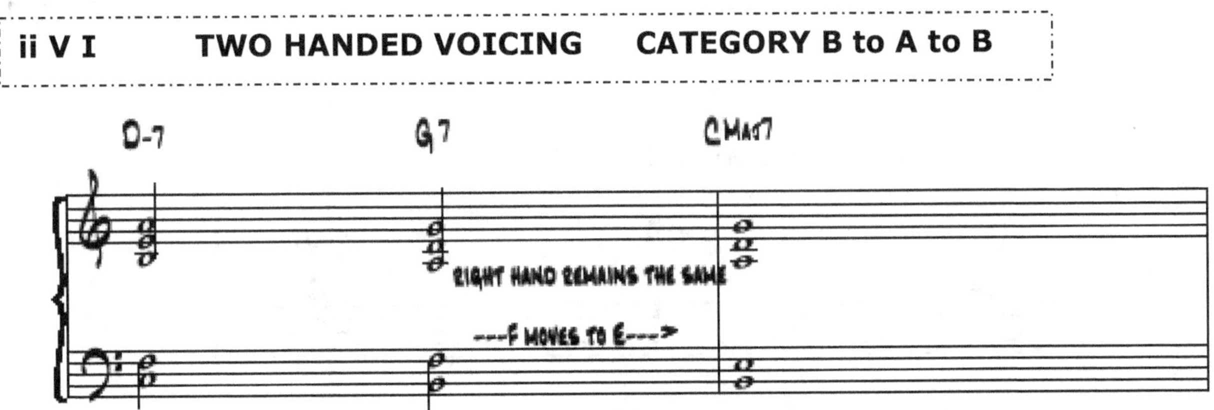

Here is this same progression in F Major.

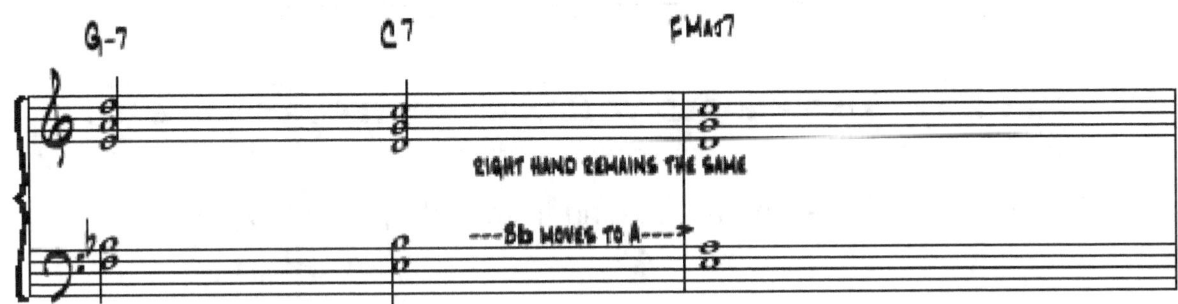

Finally, we'll look at one-handed voicings for the ii V I

Here is the progression in C Major.

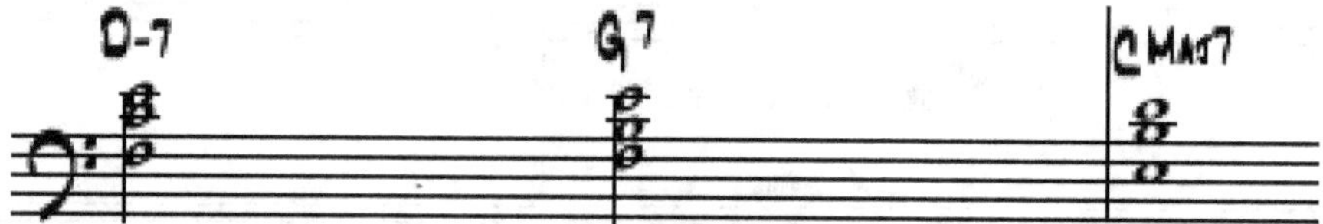

Here is the progression in F Major.

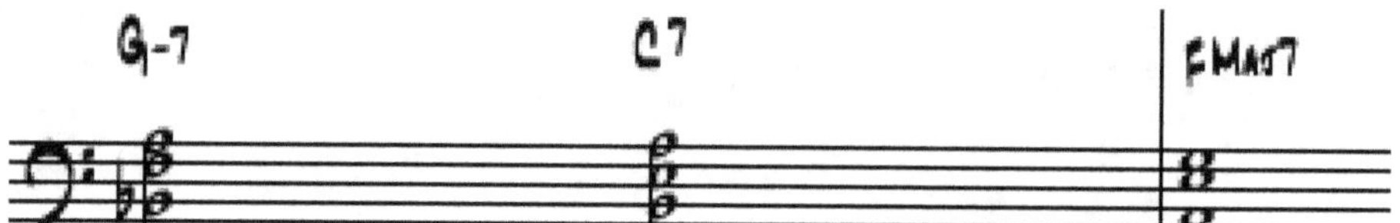

Here is the one-handed voicing from Category B to A to B.

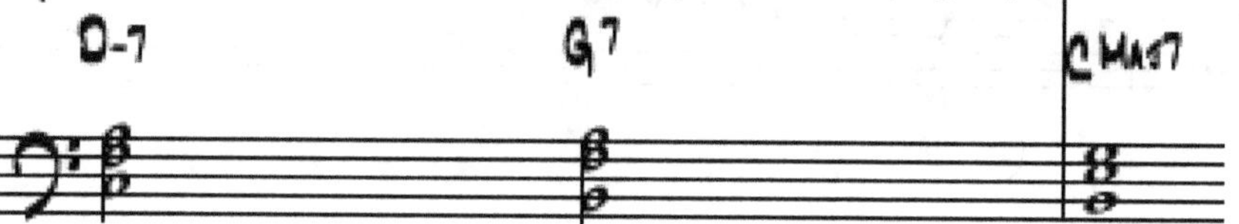

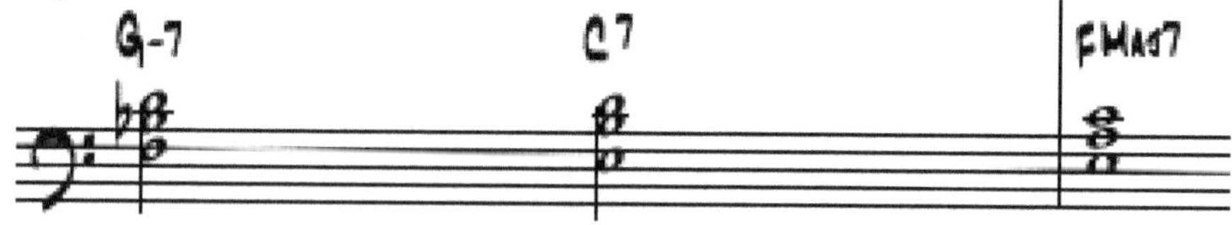

Part Two: Half-diminished and Altered Dominant Chords

Now it's time to look at some other types of chords. These two types of chords are part of the minor ii V i.

In the Minor ii V I, the ii chord will be a m7b5 chord. This type of chord is often called a "half-diminished" chord.

Let's start with the two handed m7b5 chord. We are again going to look at two different half-diminished voicings.

<table><tr><td>MINOR 7 b5</td><td>TWO HANDED VOICING</td></tr></table>

The first set of voicings has the root on the bottom:

C-7b5

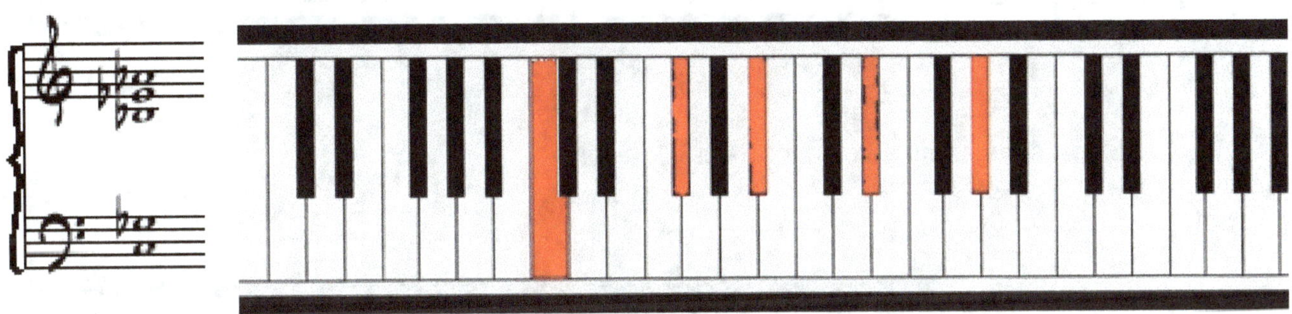

F-7b5

Tricks of the Trade

Notice that this voicing is the same as the "Category A" dominant voicing a raised 5th up.
For instance:
Our C half-diminished chord is the same as the voicing for G#7

Here is the second set of half-diminished voicings.

MINOR 7 b5   **TWO HANDED VOICING**

Let's look at the voicing for **C-7b5**

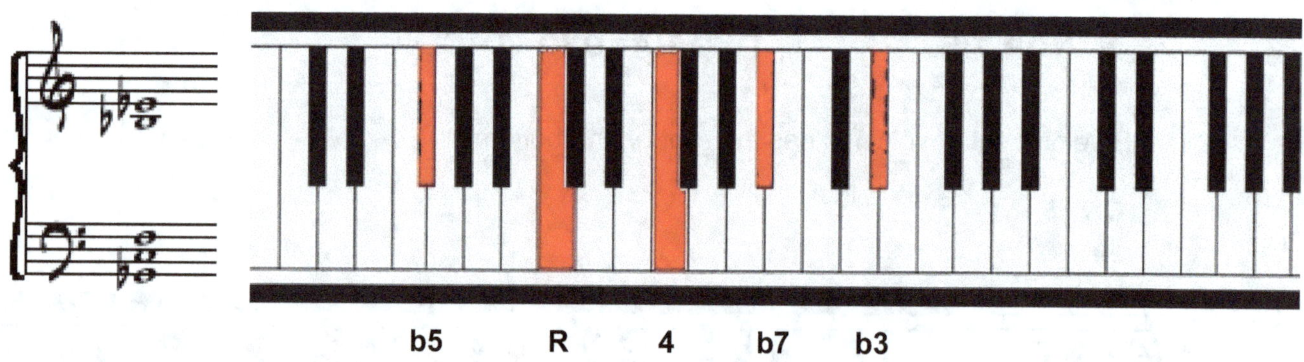

Here is the same voicing for **F-7b5**

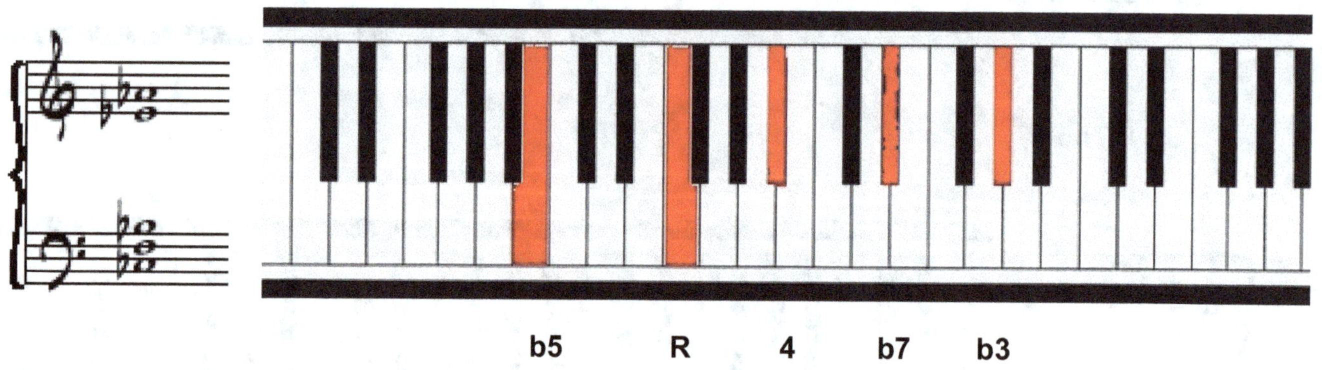

Tricks of the Trade

Notice that this voicing is the same as the "Category B" dominant voicing
a raised 5th up.
For instance:
Our C half-diminished chord is the same as the voicing for G#7
Our F half-diminished voicing is the same as the voicing for C#7

Altered Chords

Next we are going to look at the voicings for altered chords. You can play these voicings when you see the symbols C7alt, C7#9, C7#9#5

Here is the voicing for C7alt

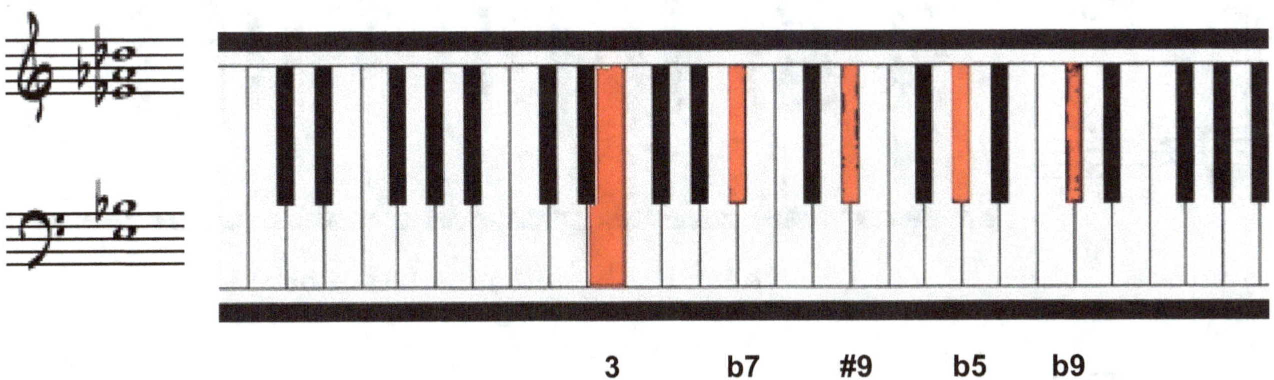

Here is this same voicing for F7alt:

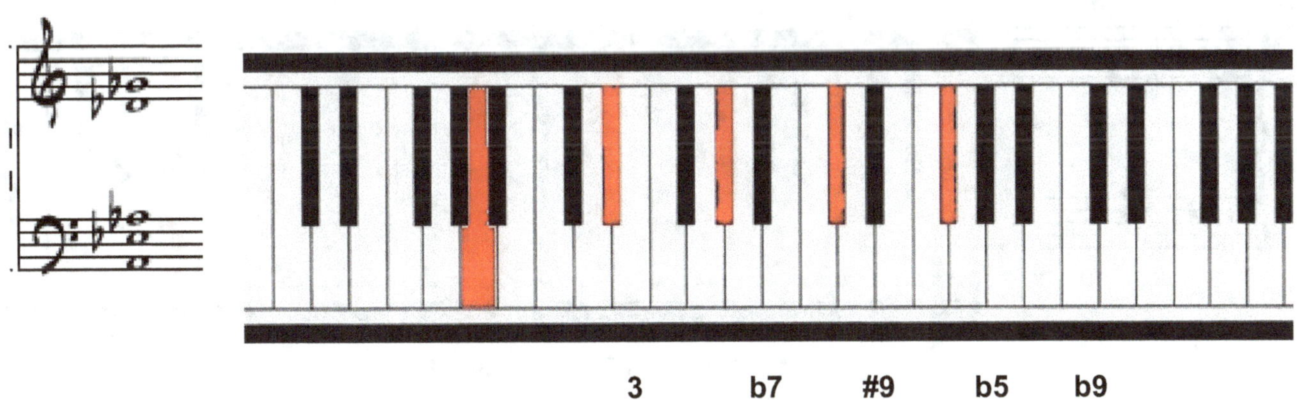

Tricks of the Trade

To form C7alt, play a C dominant 7th "CATEGORY A" voicing.
Then, raise the right hand (top three notes) up ½ a step.

C7alt

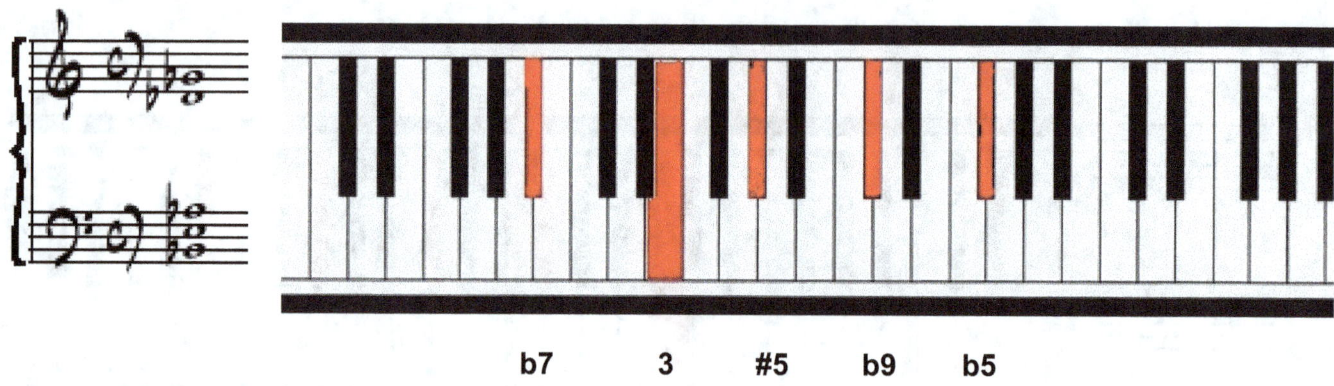

F7alt

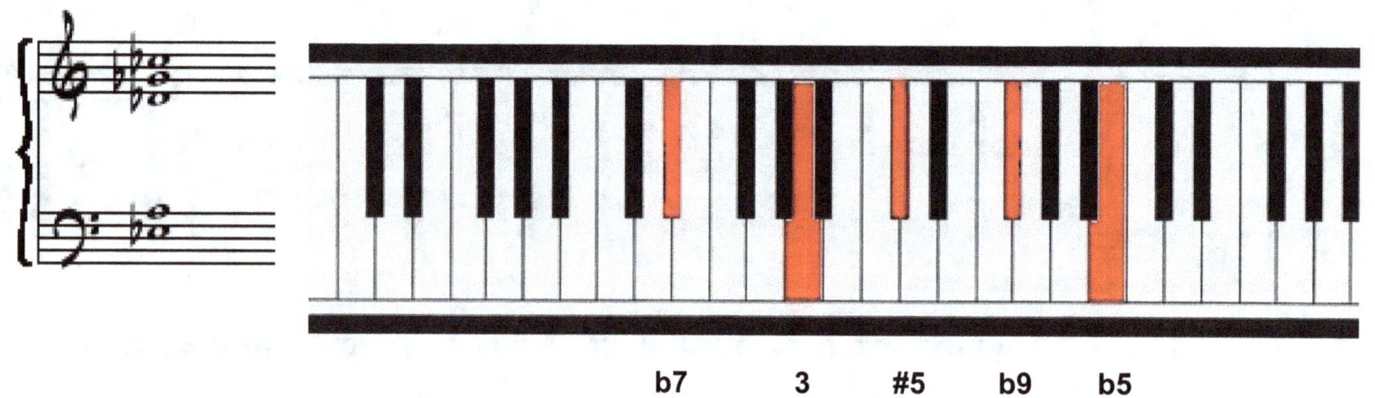

Tricks of the Trade

To form C7alt, play a C dominant 7th "Category B" voicing.
Then, LOWER the right hand (top three notes) by ½ a step.

C-7b5

F-7b5

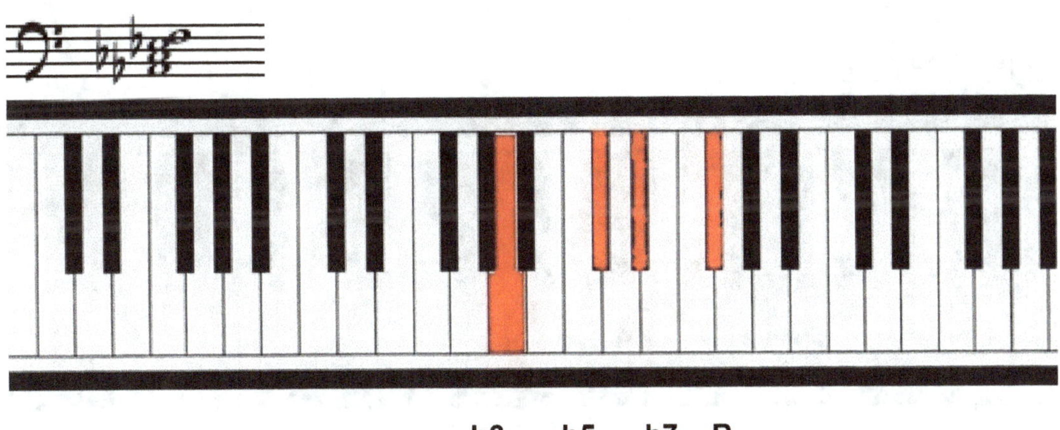

C-7b5

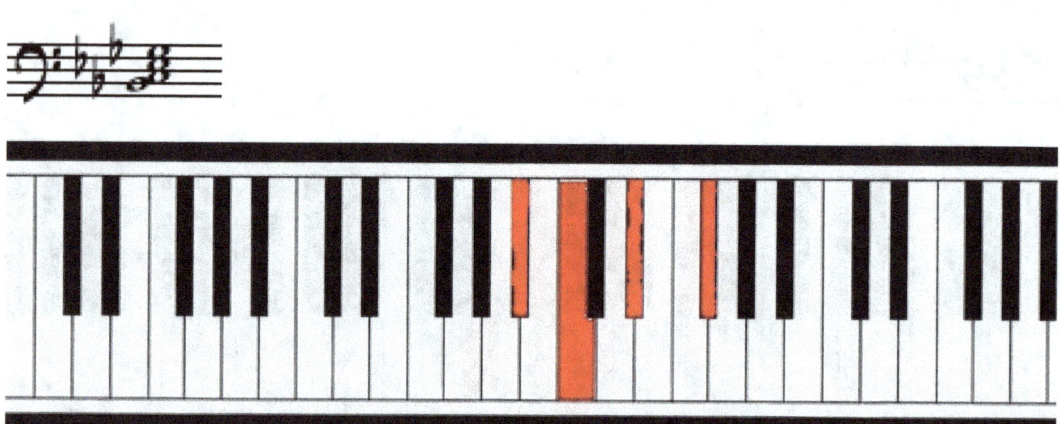

F-7b5

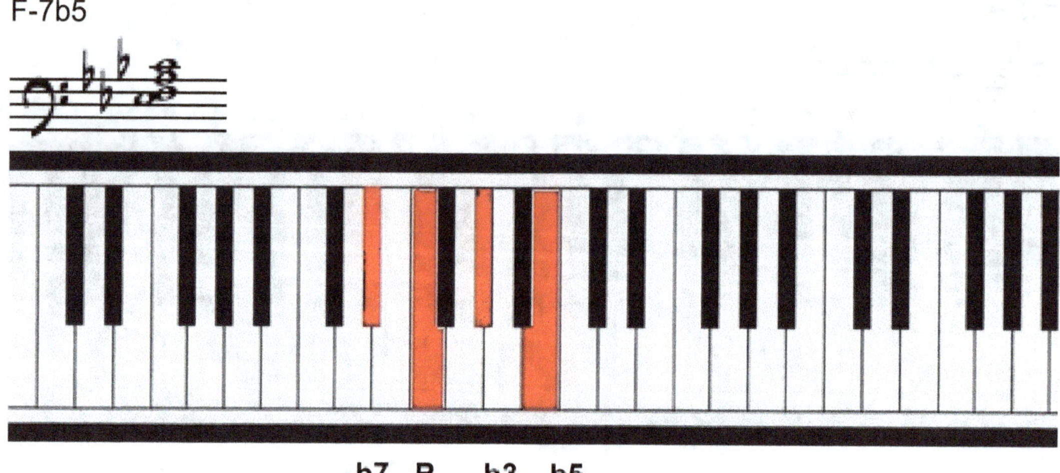

C7alt

F7alt

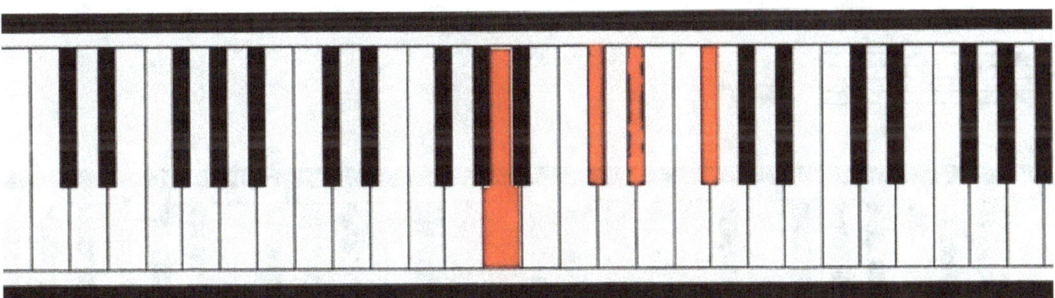

C7alt

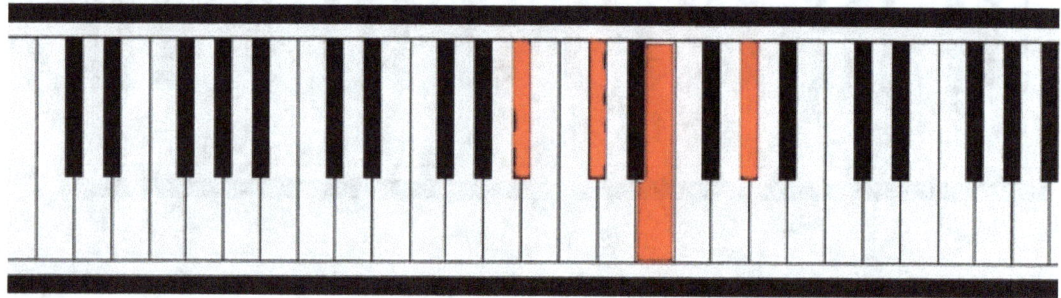

F7alt

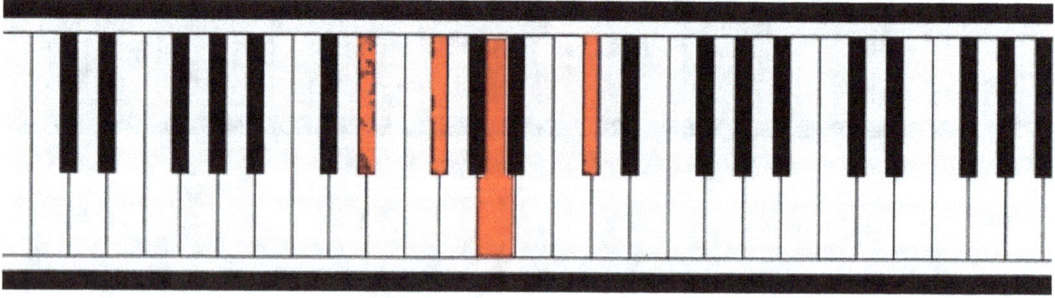

The minor ii V i

Let's put these voicings to use!

In two handed voicings, you will have to jump from the ii chord to the V chord.

The minor ii V i in c minor:

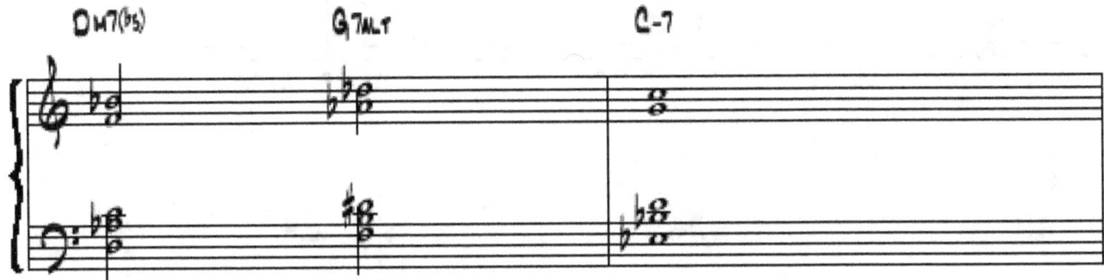

The minor ii V I in f minor.

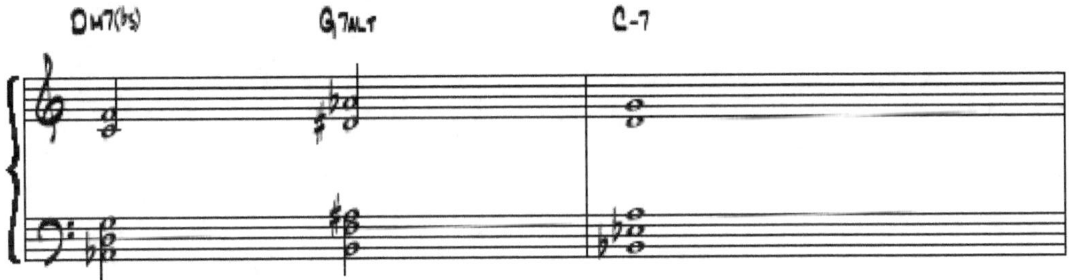

For one handed minor ii V I voicings, we are again either going to go from
category A to B to A, or from B to A to B.

You can think of sliding your forefinger and thumb each out a half of step when
moving from the ii chord to the altered dominant chord.

Here is a minor ii V I in c minor.

Other Voicings

Finally, we are going to look at some other chord voicings.

Diminished Chord (Co or Do)

Diminished chords are made out of all minor thirds.

The one- handed voicing for a diminished chord, is just this: all minor thirds.

Here is one possibly C dim voicing.

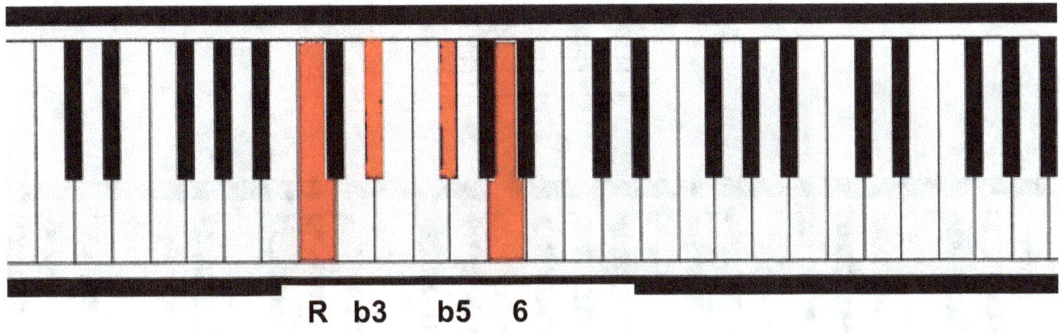

This same voicing can be played in any inversion. Here are all the inversions for C dimished:

Two Handed Diminished Voicing

To make a two handed diminished voicing, put the root on the bottom. You'll have a tri-tone in each hand, with a minor 3rd in between hands.

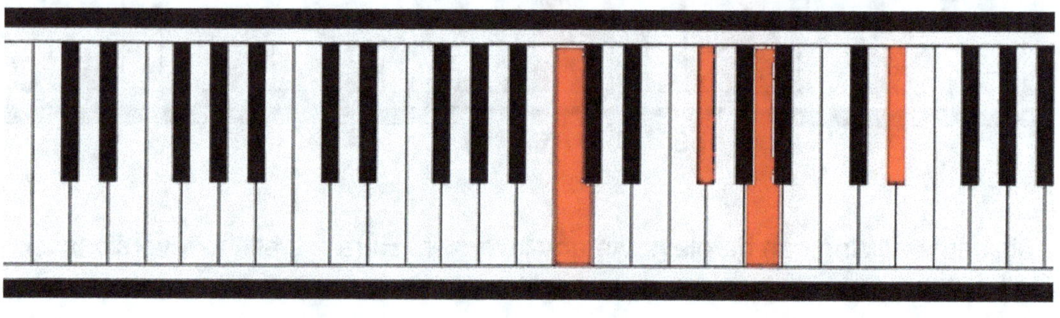

Sus Chords

For sus chords, we don't need any more voicings. Instead, play the minor 7th chord a 5th up. So, for C7sus, play a G-7 chord, and for F7sus, play a C-7 chord. Here are the voicings for C7sus and F7sus.

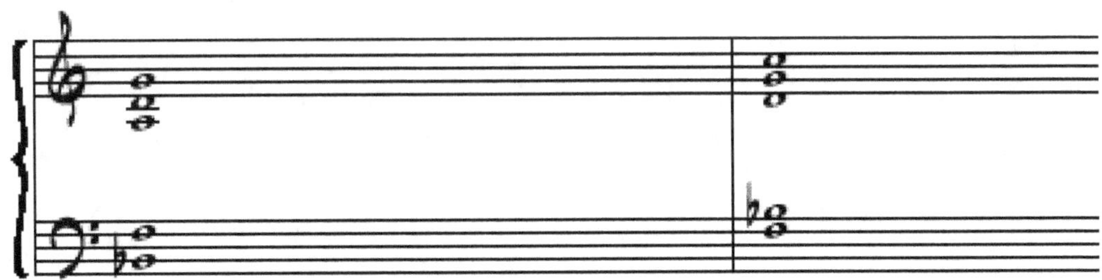

Here are two one-handed voicings for C7sus. These are the same as our G-7 one-handed voicings.

Dominant 7b9 Chords

For Dominant 7 b9 chords, use a diminished voicing from any chord tone but the root.
So, for C7b9, you can play a diminished voicing from either E, G, Bb or Db (b9). These voicings work for both one-handed and two-handed voicings.

Here are four possibilities for C7b9:

Songwriting

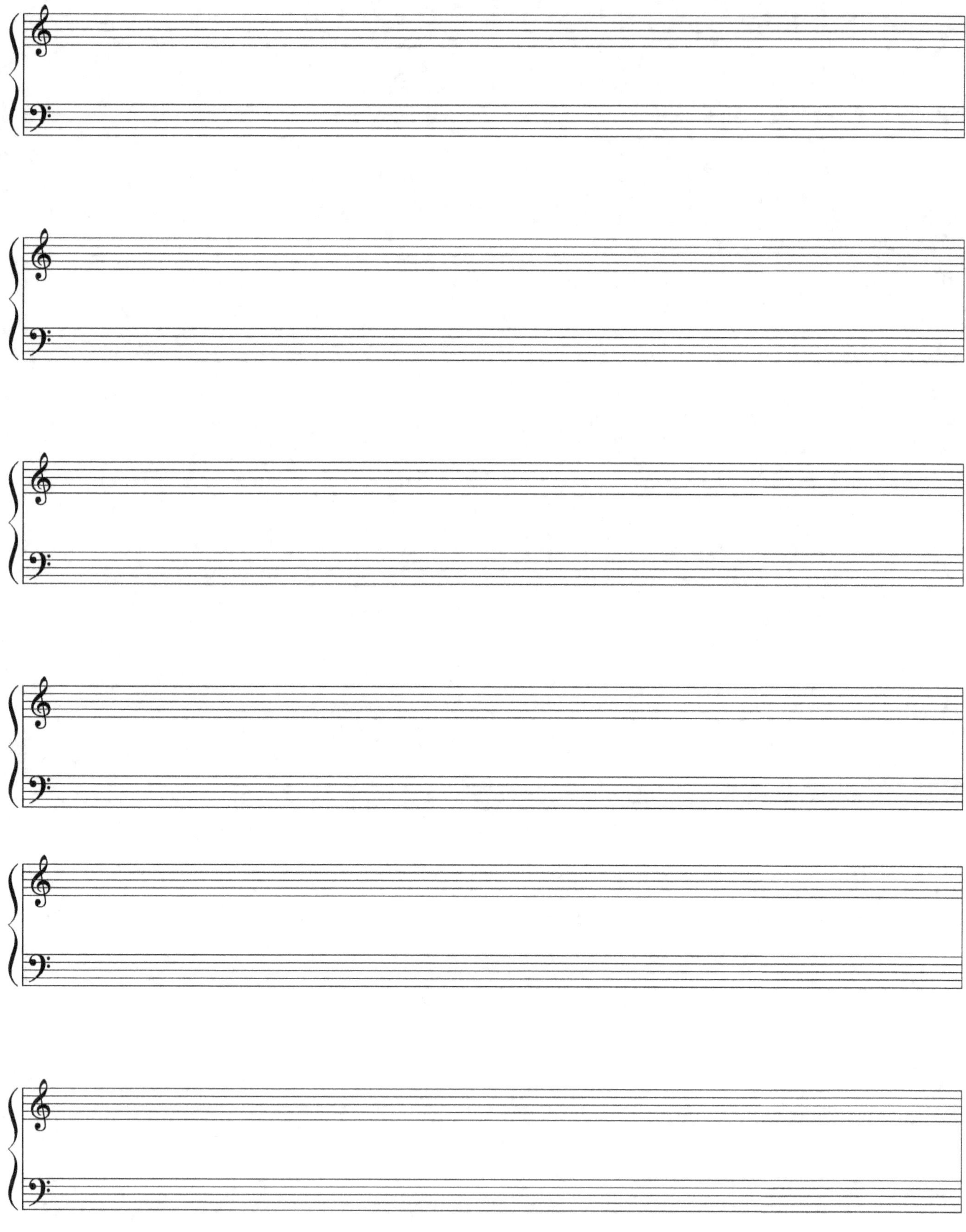

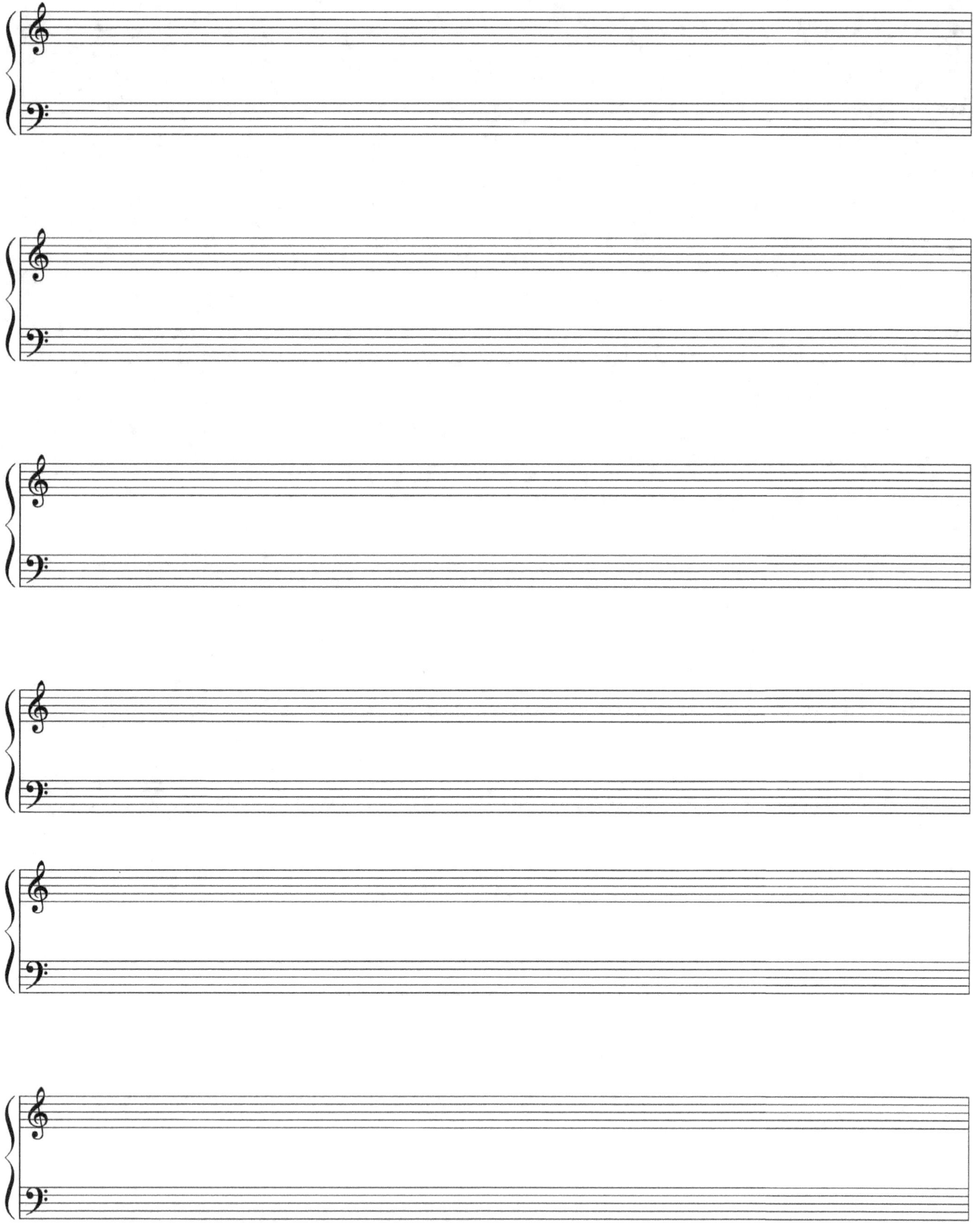

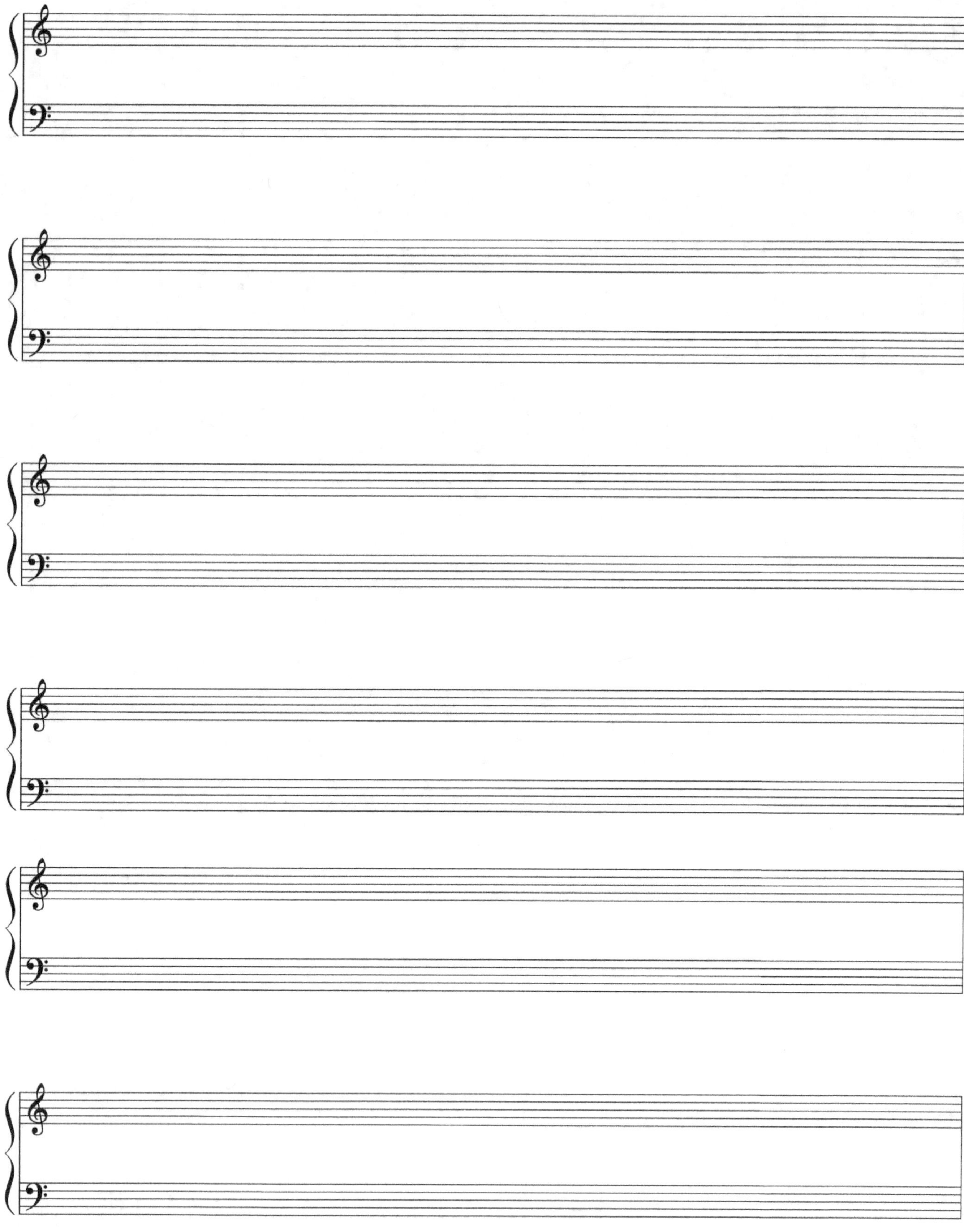

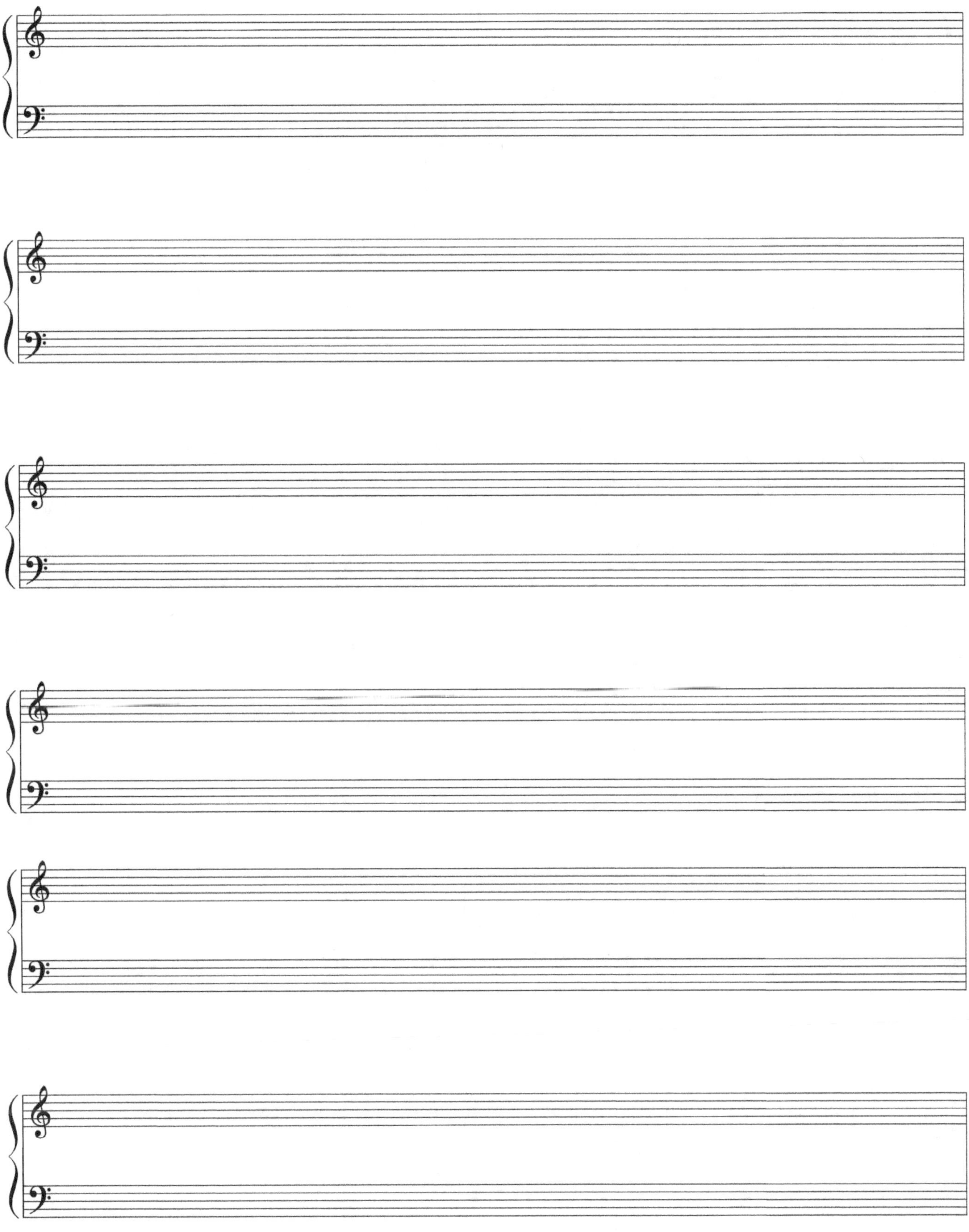

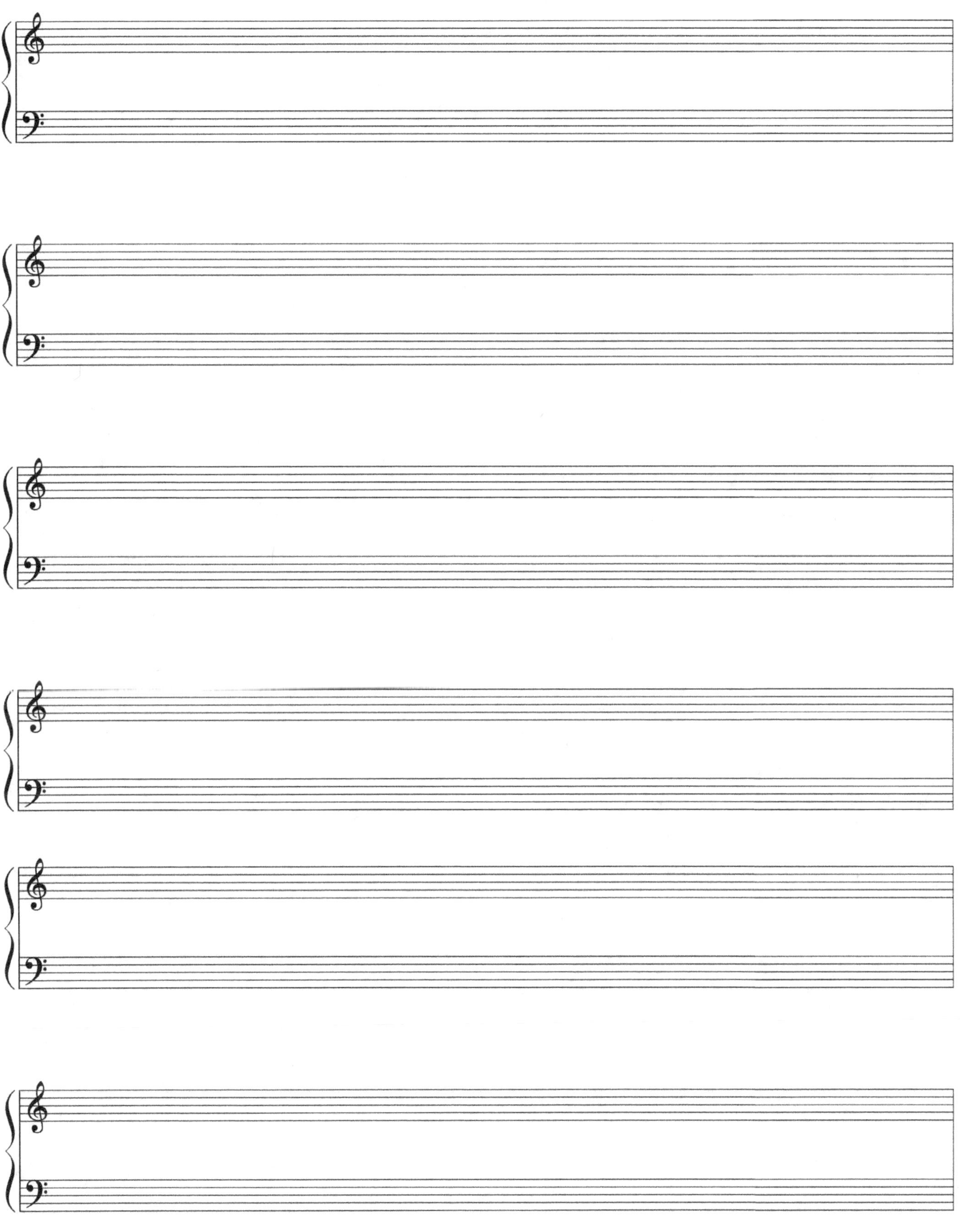

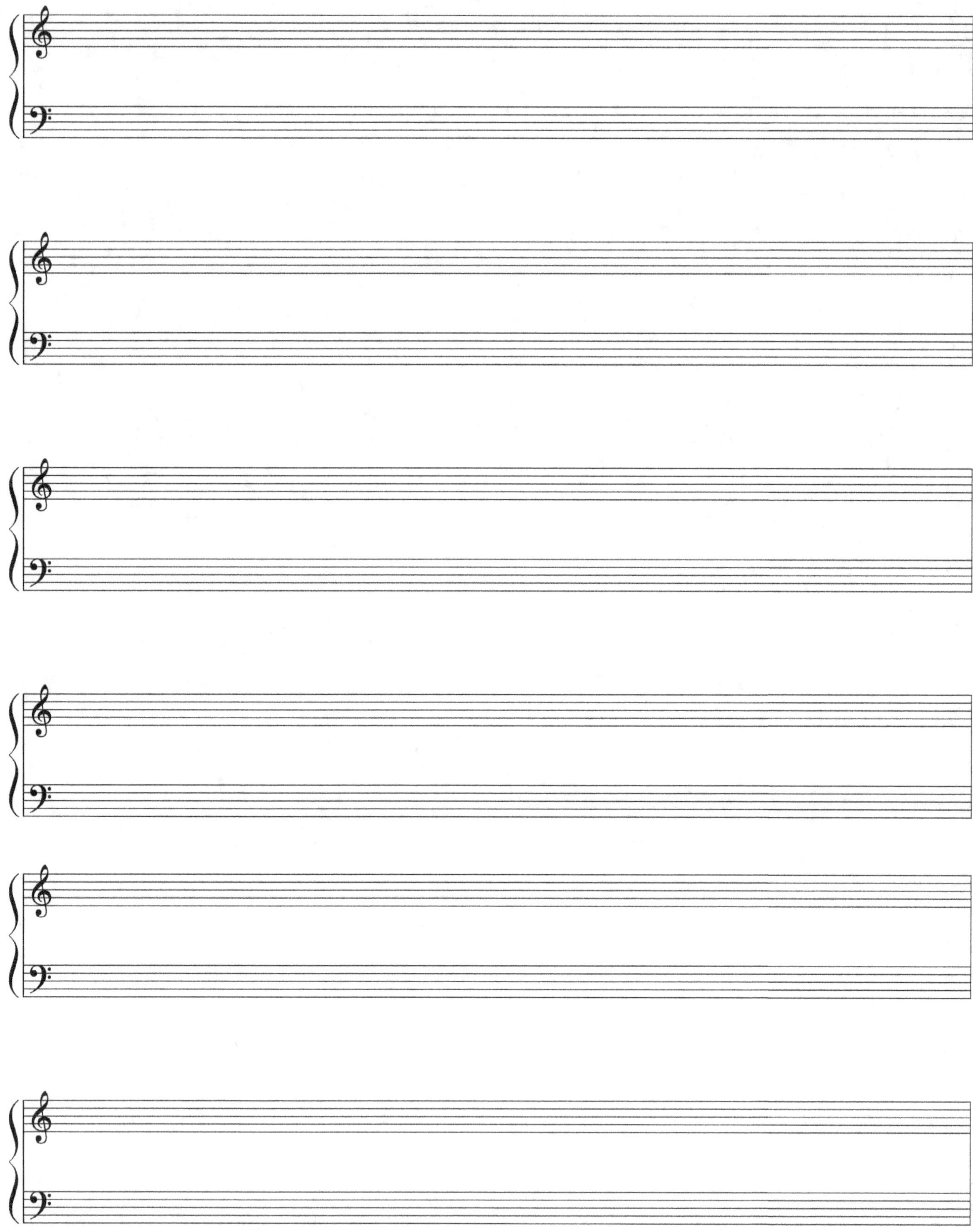

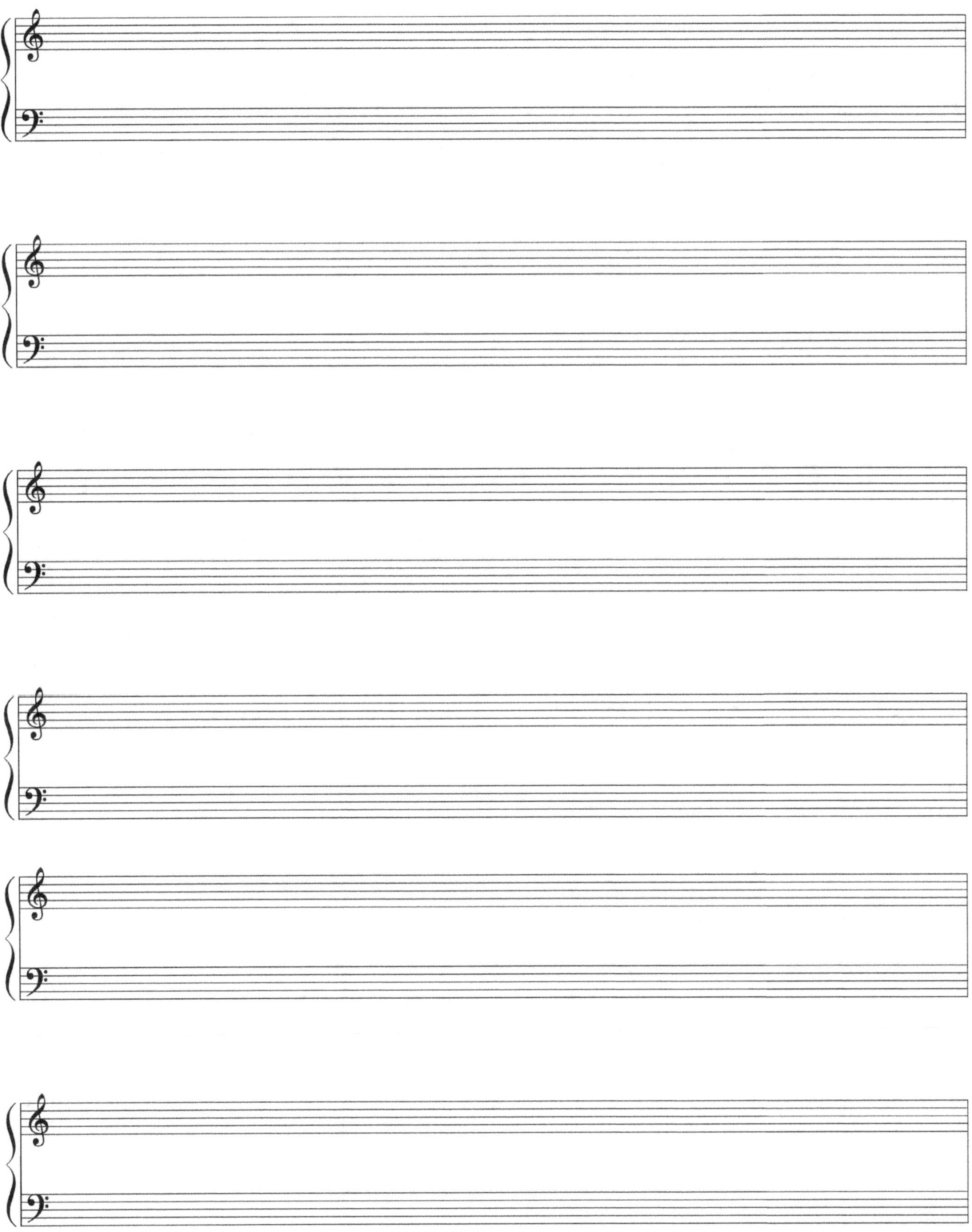

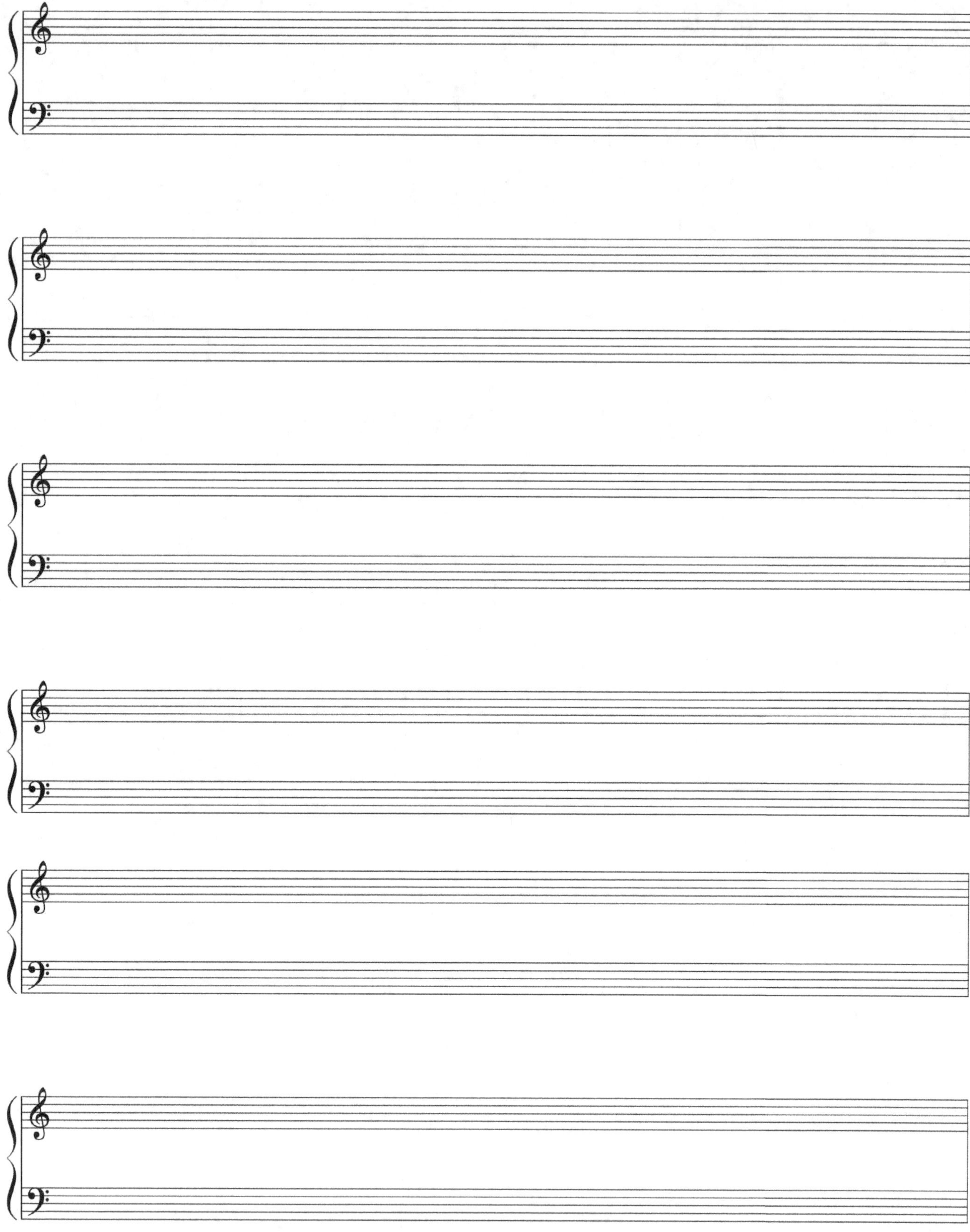

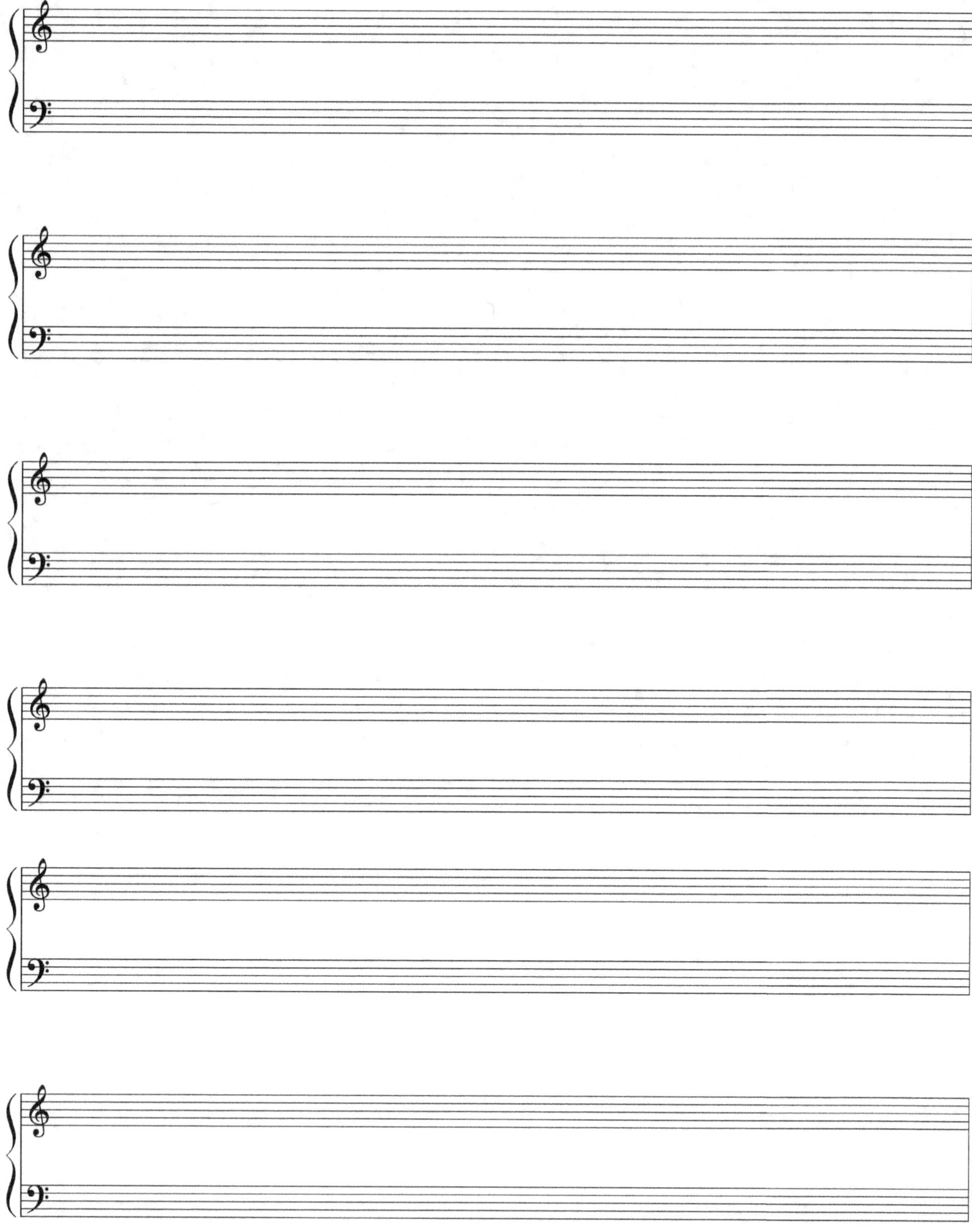

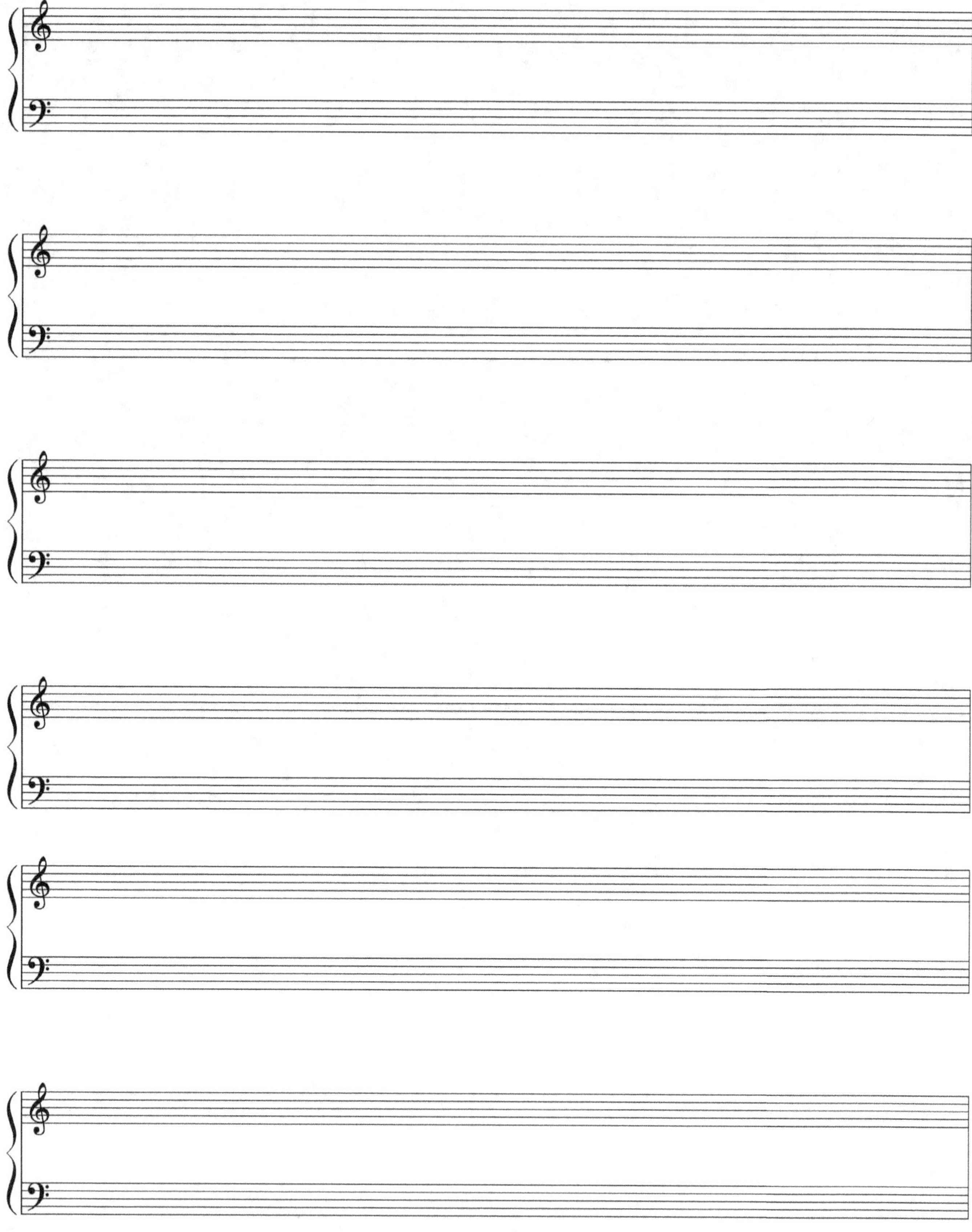

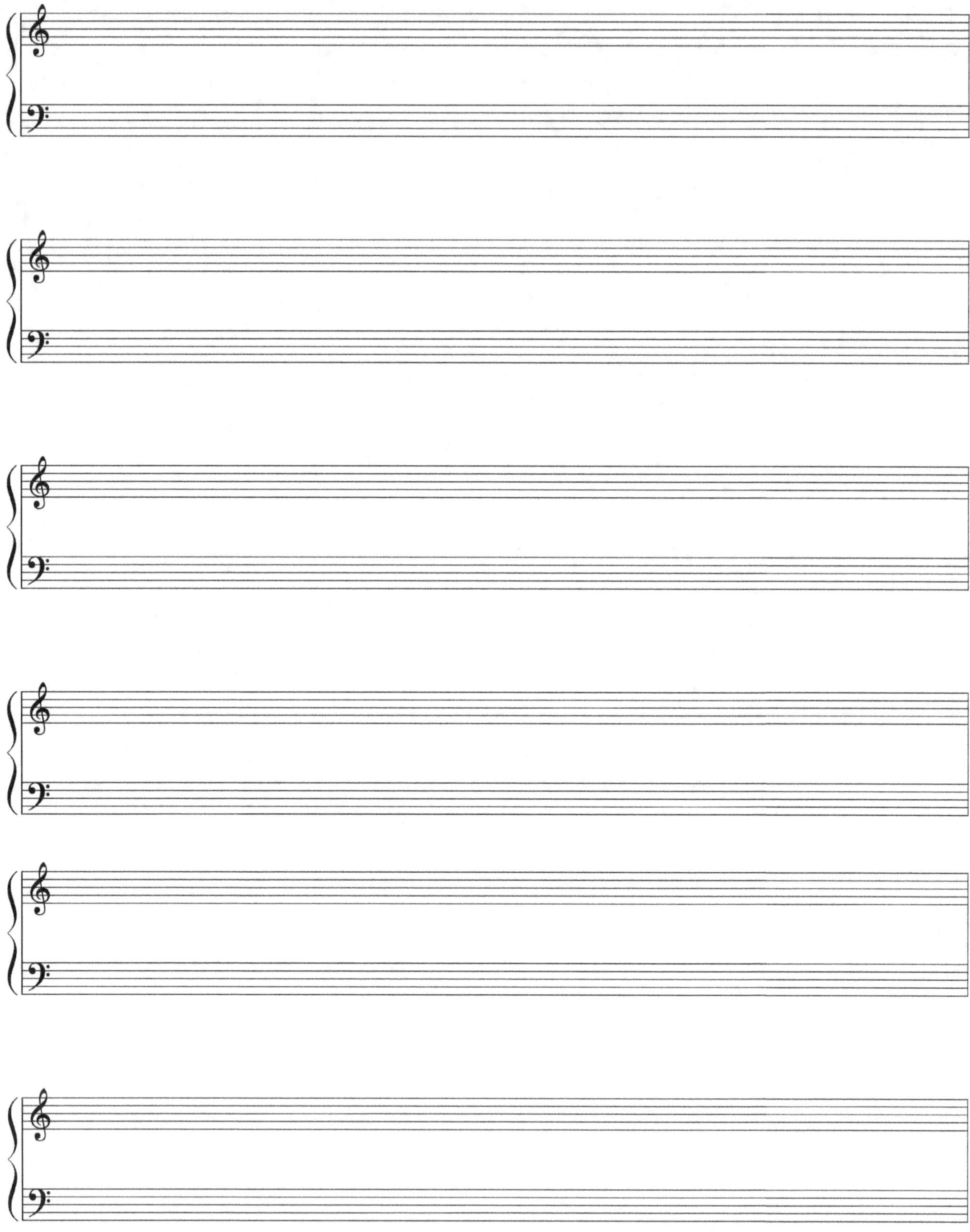

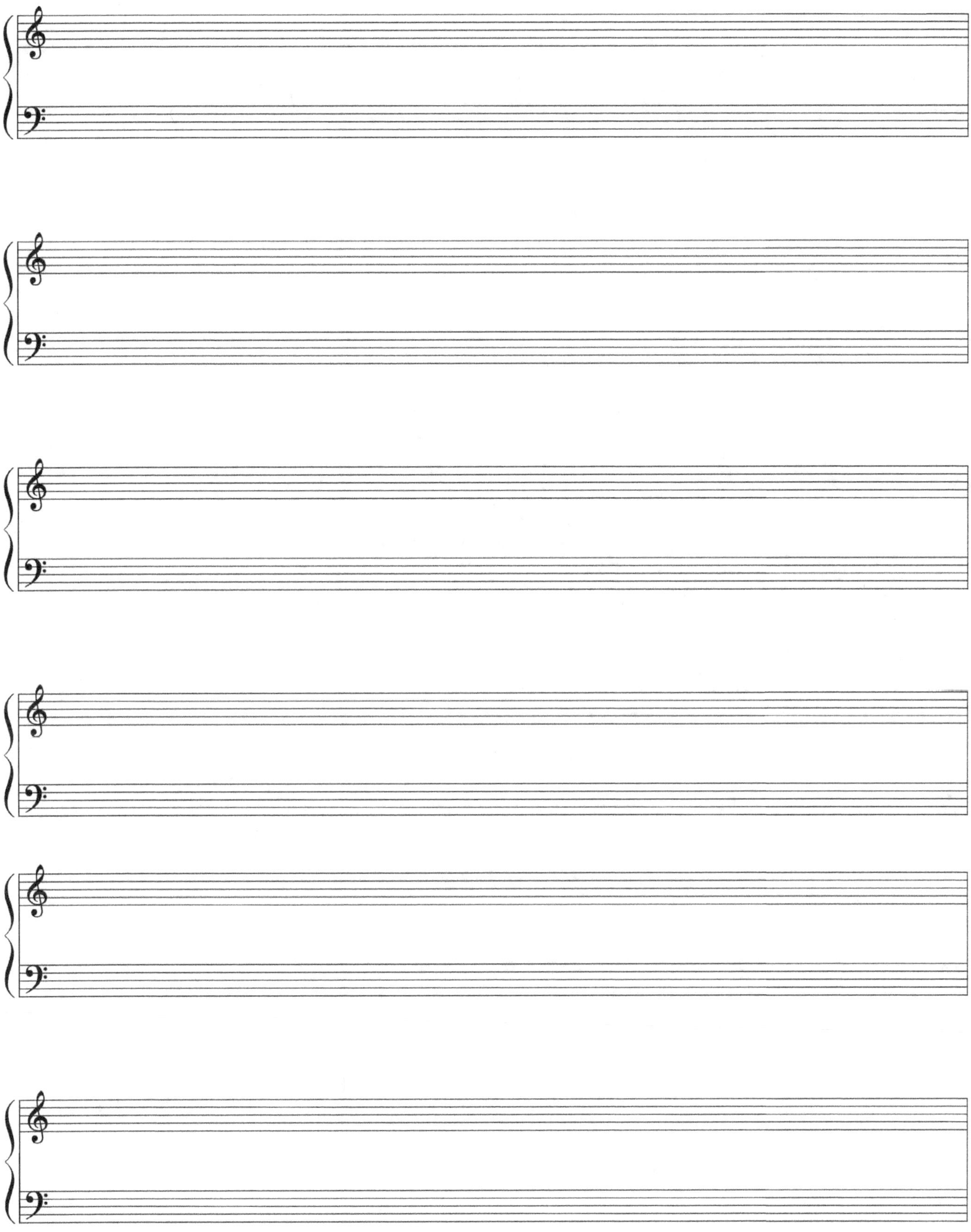

www.ingramcontent.com/pod-product-compliance
Lightning Source LLC
Chambersburg PA
CBHW060217120726
48004CB00008B/1852